MW00625109

A Guide to Colorado's Best Photography Locations

Andy Cook
Shar Scofield

Rocky Mountain Reflections Photography, Inc.
2518 Pine Bluff Road
Colorado Springs, CO 80909
www.rockymountainreflections.com
719-635-6268

Everyone should use a tripod !

COPYRIGHT

PUBLISHED BY

Rocky Mountain Reflections Photography, Inc.
2518 Pine Bluff Road
Colorado Springs, CO 80909

719-635-6268
www.rockymountainreflections.com

ISBN INFORMATION
0-9760893-0-0

All photographs taken by the author Andy Cook. Book layout and design created by Annell Allen.

NOTES

PRINTED

in Hong Kong

CONTENTS 5

INTRODUCTION

The majority of Colorado's extensive mountainous region is public property, available for various forms of recreation. Included are national forests, wildlife refuges and Bureau of Land Management holdings, as well as numerous state and local parks. For many years I have enjoyed camping, hiking, hunting, fishing, four-wheeling and sightseeing in the magnificent state of Colorado. Photographing its spectacular scenery gave me just one more excuse to spend time exploring new places. I soon learned that certain localities yielded far more dramatic images than others. Compiled in this book you'll find what I consider to be some of the very best photography locations in Colorado.

Maps are an indispensable item for any traveler. The maps in this book are not to scale and eliminate tremendous amounts of detail about the areas they represent. They are included only as aids for describing routes to particular locations and for general orientation of the reader. I strongly recommend you carry detailed topographic maps both in the car and field. I have found two sets of maps to be quite useful for exploring Colorado. The "Colorado Atlas & Gazetteer" published by DeLorme Mapping, 2 DeLorme Drive, Yarmouth, ME 04096, (800-561-5105) (www.delorme.com) is a book of topographic maps for the entire state. It sells for about $15 in most bookstores, grocery, drug and sporting goods stores throughout Colorado.

The other set of maps I rely on are Trails Illustrated maps published by National Geographic, (800-962-1643 www.trailsillustrated.com). These waterproof, tear-resistant maps fold and fit neatly in a camera pack. Each map costs approximately $10 and covers only a specific area. It often takes two or three maps to cover the region you're exploring, but I like them for hiking trails and navigating with the SUV because of their detail and ease in reading. They're not as widely available, but can often be found in outfitters such as REI and other large sporting goods retailers. The maps are numbered and organized by area. Throughout this book, I will refer to the number(s) of the map(s) you will find useful.

If you're renting a vehicle during your visit to Colorado, I strongly recommend an SUV, pick-up truck or other high-clearance vehicle. Four-wheel drive capability may also come in handy. Many locations have roads to them, but they're generally dirt with varying conditions. A high-clearance vehicle may save the day even if it's only required for short distances.

Map of Colorado

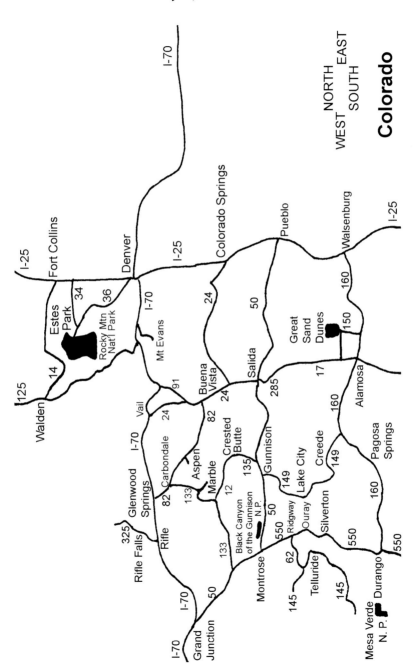

Mountain Wild

lowers

Robinson Basin

Mountain Wildflowers

Mountain Wildflowers - The peak of Colorado's mountain wildflower season is usually between the second full week and the third full week in July. Peak season varies from location to location and year to year, but if you're in the mountains during mid-July, you will be delighted with the wildflower display. Numerous natural factors such as the amount of rainfall, depth of snow pack and the season's temperatures influence exactly when flowers will peak and how sensational they might be at different locations.

During normal and cool, moist years, flowers may be found throughout Colorado, but will be especially prominent at the locations in this guide. In warm, dry years, flowers are less prevalent, but should still be found in ample supply at the locations mentioned. If you're having difficulty locating flowers during a warm, dry summer explore higher elevations, particularly above timberline, along streams and in shady areas. You should seek places that receive less direct sun as a result of the topography, such as north-facing slopes or the bottom of a narrow wash or canyon. This is where you're likely to find healthier, more vibrant flowers. Regardless of the moisture or coolness of a particular summer, many species that may be abundant near timberline are not present several hundred feet above timberline; instead an entirely new assortment of flowers may exist.

Decades ago, before people were conservation-minded, Colorado blue columbine were practically wiped out by relentless picking. Wildflowers are now legally protected and many species have made tremendous recoveries. Please do not pick them.

Two general regions top the list as favorite Colorado wildflower locations: the area surrounding Crested Butte and the Western Region of the San Juan Mountains.

Stony Pass - Alpine sunflowers on the shoulder of Green Mountain.

Crested Butte Region

Crested Butte

Crested Butte (Trails Illustrated Maps 128, 131, 133) - For quite some time, Crested Butte has been a quirky winter ski destination of growing popularity. Recently, knowledge of its amazing collection of summer wildflowers has begun to spread. Now Crested Butte calls itself the Wildflower Capitol of Colorado — with good reason. Travel just a short distance in almost any direction and you will find yourself in awe of vast, colorful fields of mountain wildflowers. Depending upon the conditions of the year, you may simply drive some of the more obvious roads in the area and find ample flowers for plentiful roadside shooting. However, there are times when the flowers are not so apparent and detailed information about specific hot spots is required to fill the numerous rolls of film carried by most anticipating photographers. Following are some of my favorite Crested Butte locations that have yielded productive shooting year after year.

Where to stay in the Crested Butte region? I usually lodge in Crested Butte, a quaint summer tourist destination surrounded by breathtaking mountains. The town has lodging, shopping and restaurants. Occasionally, I stay in Gunnison, a larger town 45 minutes south of Crested Butte. Gunnison is a tidy college town with several motels, but it's surrounded by uninteresting rolling sagebrush hills. Use the following website and phone number to help make lodging/camping reservations:

Crested Butte
Chamber of Commerce
800-545-4505
www.crestedbuttechamber.com

Crested Butte, Colorado. Taken at dawn, late July.

Map of Crested Butte Area

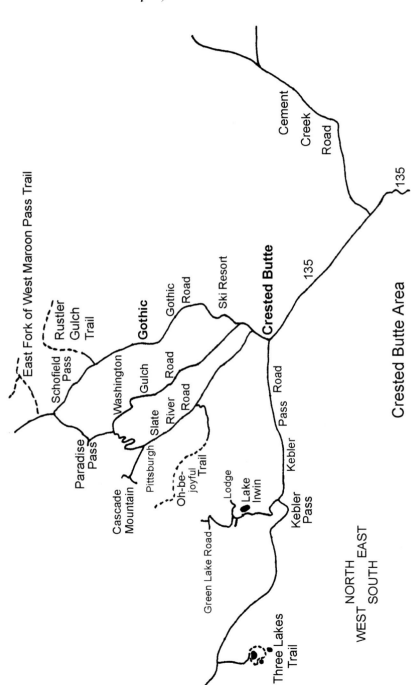

Crested Butte Area

Lake Irwin Area

This area is relatively easy to access and has some of the best wildflower shooting in the Crested Butte region. Listed below are two routes worth exploring. **Directions**: Travel west out of Crested Butte on County Road 12 (Kebler Pass Road) toward Kebler Pass. Go about 6 miles and just before the pass, turn right (north) on Country

Road 826 (Lake Irwin Road) toward Lake Irwin. Some years, as you climb through the woods toward the lake, you may find significant patches of wildflowers along the road. If not, don't despair. Drive past the lake and campground, which you'll pass on your right, and proceed uphill. As you break out of the trees, about 1/4 mile beyond the campground, start looking for flowers. The road may get a little rough and a high-clearance vehicle or four-wheel drive may be necessary. From this point you have two options:

Colorado blue columbine and waterfall on the west side of Green Lake Road in Robinson Basin. Taken midafternoon, late July.

1) Proceed to the first left turn which travels only a short distance to a trailhead. Sneezeweed and fairies trumpet are usually common along this short drive.

2) Proceed to the second left on Forest Road 826.1E (Green Lake Road) which will twist and turn its way up into the high west flank of Robinson Basin, a wonderful area with streams, waterfalls, numerous flowers, small ponds, mountain backdrops and unlimited shooting possibilities. **Note**: The left hand turn for this road is just before the gate to Lake Irwin Lodge. As you drive the first section of it, you will be passing through private property and it may appear that you are using someone's driveway since the road travels very close to several structures. **If I could visit only one place in the Crested Butte region, this would be it**. This road does require four-wheel drive, but is relatively easy and not precipitous. If you do not have a four-wheel drive vehicle, consider parking on the side of the road where it becomes too difficult to drive and continue on foot. In less than one mile along this road you will find waterfalls and colorful fields of flowers. Many flowers are represented in this area with columbine being one of the most common. I prefer to shoot waterfalls and cascades in the shade, therefore, I recommend shooting this area in the afternoon when the mountain itself shades the cascades and waterfalls.

Photography Tip: Cloudy, overcast days are excellent for photographing close-ups and small flower groups. Your eyes may not agree with this, but film sees things differently. The diffused light provides the very best illumination to reveal fine flower details and saturated color. If you wish to photograph a grand landscape and include flowers in the composition, shoot it in early morning or late afternoon; at these times sunlight travels through more of the earth's atmosphere and takes on a softer nature.

When shooting wildflowers, I find three filters very handy for controlling light and capturing what I see on film. I make extensive use of Singh-Ray's color intensifier (for warm colors — yellow, orange, red). I often use a polarizer and occasionally a warming filter. For details about these filters and their use see page 128.

Assortment of flowers near the beginning of Green Lake Road.
Taken midafternoon, late July.

Gothic Road

Gothic Road (Forest Road 317) - Gothic Road will take you past large stands of aspen, their slender trunks mingling with many white cow parsnip flowers and fields of purple fireweed — all before you reach the small settlement named Gothic. During the summer this road is maintained and passable by car. **Directions**: In Crested Butte, State Hwy 135 ends, but the road continues and is called Gothic Road. Drive it from the town of Crested Butte toward the ski resort, about 2 miles. Follow through the resort. As you leave the dense housing area, the road turns to dirt. In about 6 miles you'll reach the small settlement of Gothic. Often, depending upon weather conditions, additional fields of flowers may be found further up Forest Road 317 toward Schofield Pass.

Fireweed growing along Gothic Road.

Washington Gulch Road

Washington Gulch Road (Forest Road 811) - This road will take you up the gentle slope of a mountain and into beautiful wildflower country where you can expect to find a wide variety of flowers including columbine, bluebells and sneezeweed. There are a few areas of posted, private land along stretches of this road. Please respect the wishes of property owners and obey signs. Much of this road is passable by car. However, the higher you climb, the more likely you'll encounter rough sections of road requiring the higher clearance of a two-wheel drive pick-up or SUV. Flowers are generally more abundant at the higher elevations. **Directions**: From Crested Butte, head toward the ski resort on Gothic Road (only road leading to the resort) and turn left onto Washington Gulch Road just before you reach the resort, about 1.75 miles from Crested Butte. There is a street sign here.

Tall chiming bells along Washington Gulch Road

Slate River Road

Slate River Road (Forest Road 734) - Approximately 4 miles up this road you'll pass a winter closure gate. Depending upon the season, you may find flowers as you near the gate; if it's been a dry, hot year, you may have to drive further up the road. During cool, moist years, columbine may be abundant; in warm, dry years, sneezeweed will likely be more prolific. Much of this road is passable by car. However, as you increase in elevation, a high-clearance vehicle such as a two-wheel drive pick-up or SUV may be required. **Directions**: From the town of Crested Butte, head toward the ski resort on Gothic Road (only road leading to the resort). Travel about 2/3 mile; take the first left turn onto Slate River Road, marked by a street sign.

A misty morning about 4 miles up Slate River Road near Crested Butte.
Taken at dawn, late July.

Note: Slate River Road and Washington Gulch Road connect high on the mountain, about 11 or 12 miles depending on route, and continue up to **Paradise Pass**, another 1.25 miles. (One map refers to the road approaching the pass as Washington Gulch Road, but both maps number it Forest Road 734.) Following this route over Paradise Pass and down the north side, you will connect with Gothic Road, which this far north is called Schofield Pass Road.

Cement Creek Road

Cement Creek Road (Forest Road 740) - Cement Creek is less frequently visited and can yield a variety of flowers including lupine, paintbrush and elephants head. Most flowers will be found near and above timberline. There will be a small creek above timberline about 40 yards west of the road. It's in a shallow ravine and not visible from the road. Many flowers can usually be found along this creek. Avoid areas with lots of willow as it can be tough to walk through, especially with camera equipment, and it's unproductive territory because willow tends to choke out most competing plants and flowers. **Directions**: Drive south from Crested Butte on State Hwy 135 for about 6 miles, turn left onto Cement Creek Road. The first 8 or 9 miles is easy driving, but shortly after the Italian Creek Road junction, the condition of the road deteriorates, requiring four-wheel drive. In about 4 more miles you should start seeing shooting possibilities with good potential continuing for the next 2 or 3 miles to the end of the road. I caution against driving to the very end as it becomes treacherous. Once you're above timberline, I recommend parking and walking — it's always the best way to see flowers.

Paintbrush and elephants head along Cement Creek

Photography Tip: Shooting flowers from their level often creates a more appealing composition than shooting down at them. Carefully study the flower(s) you're about to shoot. They should be fresh, brilliant and the very best specimens available. Avoid photographing tired, blemished or torn flowers. Why? Because the viewer's eye will notice defects and focus on them, detracting from your intended subject.

Trails of the Crested Butte Region to Hike and Photograph

Rustler Gulch Trail

Rustler Gulch Trail - The trail is relatively easy to hike with a gradual uphill climb. Stream crossings without bridges will be your greatest challenge. Columbine, paintbrush, sneezeweed and many other flowers are common near and above timberline. **Directions**: From Crested Butte, drive Gothic Road toward the ski resort (only road leading to the resort). Follow it through the resort. As you leave the dense housing area, the road turns to dirt. In about 6 miles you will pass the town of Gothic; in another 2 miles you'll reach Gothic Campground, located on the left side of the road. Continue another 3/4 mile north of the campground, turn right on Rustler Gulch Road and proceed about 1 mile to the trailhead. This road may require a four-wheel drive vehicle, but there's room to park at the turn onto Rustler Gulch Road if you don't have a suitable vehicle.

Creek along trail in Rustler Gulch. Taken early morning in late July.

Above timberline in Rustler Gulch. Taken midmorning, late July.

East Fork of West Maroon Pass Trail

East Fork of West Maroon Pass Trail - The trail is difficult mainly because the first mile has a steady incline with a fair amount of elevation gain. The first part of the trail winds through a forest, emerging from the trees into an endless alpine meadow and vast expanse of wildflowers. As you finish the first mile you will begin to appreciate the reward for your effort as you discover the higher you climb, the more abundant the flowers become. **Directions**: Drive Gothic Road from the town of Crested Butte toward the ski resort, about 2 miles (only road leading to the resort). Follow it through the resort. As you leave the dense housing area the road turns to dirt. Continue on Gothic Road up over Schofield Pass. (Gothic Road becomes Schofield Pass Road as it approaches the pass.) As you head down the north side, go right at the fork in the road. Approximately 1/2 mile past the fork you will cross a

stream; just beyond the stream, turn right into the trailhead parking lot. The road to the trailhead is usually well-maintained and most vehicles can make it to the stream. Some people choose to park before the stream and wade across; it's only about shin deep. **Note**: Trailhead is approximately 13 miles from Crested Butte.

Paintbrush along East Fork of West Maroon Pass Trail.

Three Lakes Trail

Three Lakes Trail - This moderate trail is a loop about 2 miles long which passes three lakes. Often wildflowers are not as abundant here as the other locations; however, it's a very pleasant hike where you can expect to see fireweed and paintbrush, as well as lesser amounts of other varieties. Also, you're likely to see beaver in one or more of the lakes.

This image was photographed near Lost Lake (it's visible just above the paintbrush) facing north. Taken midmorning, late July.

When I'm enjoying a longer stay in Crested Butte, I use this hike as an opportunity to see something different and take a break from the area immediately surrounding the Butte. **Directions**: From Crested Butte, travel west out of town on County Road 12 (Kebler Pass Road). Go about 15 miles and turn left on Forest Road 706; also known as Lost Lake Road and marked by a sign for Lost Lake Campground. When you reach the campground, take the road that follows the lake shore (lake will be on your right). Make the first right onto a small peninsula and follow to the parking lot at the end. There's not a formal trailhead marker for this path; it wraps around the east side of Lost Lake Slough and is easily found by walking the shore. The parking lot is accessible by car; high-clearance vehicle not required. **Note**: As you drive through Kebler Pass on the way to this trail, you will be passing through one of the largest aspen forests in the Rocky Mountains.

One memorable day, when following the stream above Lost Lake, I narrowly escaped a tragedy. I could hear the sound of a substantial waterfall and had to see if it was worth photographing. After climbing a steep hill, I spotted the waterfall and it was a beauty! I went a little closer, took off my camera pack and with some difficulty, positioned the tripod. It was challenging due to the loose soil and steep incline, which further downhill, gave way to a thirty foot cliff and rushing stream. I unzipped the pack, removed my camera and lens and secured it to the tripod. It took awhile to compose the shot and moments after tripping the shutter, I heard a dreadful, rushing sound. I yelped in fear. I thought I was about to be overrun by some wild animal. As I turned to face my attacker, I realized the dreadful noise was my camera pack sliding down the slope toward the cliff. As it approached the thirty foot drop, it flipped up and snagged on a dead tree branch. Initially I was relieved, then horrified to discover the pack was unzipped and rearranged. I assumed some equipment must have escaped and tumbled over the cliff into the water. After retrieving and reorganizing my pack, I realized just how fortunate I was. Only a lens cap and unexposed roll of film was lost. The experience motivates me to offer these words of caution: When in the field shooting, after you've removed equipment from your pack, always close and zip it, especially when on an incline.

Oh-Be-Joyful Trail

Oh-Be-Joyful Trail - As with most wildflower locations in the region, when you reach timberline and above, you can expect to find a large variety of species. **Directions**: To reach the trailhead from Crested Butte, take Gothic Road toward the ski resort. In approximately 2/3 mile, turn left on Slate River Road and follow for about 4.5 miles where you'll find an open meadow area. Look for a sharp-angled, left-hand turn; heading downhill this left turn is well-signed. As you drive down toward the stream, you will notice it's a popular camping area. Cross the stream and veer left just after crossing. You will notice the road then splits and rejoins in several hundred feet. From here, it's a four-wheel drive road that can get pretty rough. Many people park at the stream, wade through the water (usually about knee deep), and hike the road to the trailhead. The trailhead can be tricky to spot, so here are a few clues to help you find it: When the 4-wd road starts petering out at the bottom of an avalanche chute, it veers left. As it turns left, look for the trail on the right side of the road. The first 3.5 miles of this trail is relatively easy with about 1000 feet of elevation gain and will yield wildflower opportunities early in the season. The next 1.5 miles is more difficult with an elevation gain of about 1,500 feet, but will lead you into Democrat Basin with its abundant wildflowers and magnificent scenery.

Democrat Basin taken late morning in July.

Photography Tip: Is it a bright, sunny day and you want to shoot a clump of wildflowers? Use a diffuser to create better photography illumination. To find out more about diffusers, see page 138.

Other Scenic Shooting Locations of the Crested Butte Region

Paradise Pass

Paradise Pass - Dawn is a great time for shooting mountain reflections in the small ponds here. In the evening, consider climbing partially up Cinnamon Mountain, located on the west side of Paradise Pass. The views to the northeast from the shoulder of this mountain are spectacular and can be photographed well in the evening as sunset approaches. **Directions**: To reach Paradise Pass from Crested Butte, take Gothic Road toward the ski resort. Go about 1.75 miles, turn left on Washington Gulch Road (Forest Road 811), marked by a street sign. Follow for about 10 miles to its highest point. You'll find a pond on the left; just beyond it, veer left at the fork and park alongside the road. Walk the left fork several hundred feet until you see another small pond on your left. For additional, smaller ponds, follow downhill about 75 yards. **Note**: You'll likely need the high-clearance of a pick-up or SUV to reach this location.

Paradise Pass view to the north from shoulder of Cinnamon Mountain.

This is one of the small ponds atop Paradise Pass. This image was photographed from four inches above the ground. Taken at sunrise, late July.

Lupine and paintbrush in Paradise Pass. Taken early morning in late July.

Washington Gulch Road

Scenic view from Washington Gulch Road - The lush green of this expansive view is unusual for Colorado and will photograph best in morning light. **Directions**: Several hundred yards down from Paradise Pass (see directions on page 25 to Paradise Pass), heading toward Crested Butte, you will be delighted by a fantastic view of Slate River Valley and mountains to both the south and west. There's not much space to pull your vehicle off the road here so shoot fast to avoid blocking traffic, or pull over above or below and walk along the road to find the perfect shot.

The scenic view from Washington Gulch Road. Taken midmorning, late July.

Beaver Ponds on Schofield Pass Road

Beaver Ponds on Schofield Pass Road - Near Gothic Campground, above the town of Gothic, are several beaver ponds on the East River that can yield delightful early morning photographs with mountain reflections. **Directions**: From Crested Butte, drive Gothic Road toward the ski resort (only road leading to the resort). Follow it through the resort. As you leave the dense housing area, the road turns to dirt. In about 6 miles you will pass the town of Gothic. Approximately 1.5 miles past the town of Gothic, the road will cross East River via a concrete bridge. Immediately past the bridge, turn right into a dirt parking lot. (If you reach Gothic Campground, you've missed the location by about 1/3 mile.) A two-wheel drive car can easily clear this road.

You'll notice the beaver ponds from the parking lot, but be prepared to get your feet wet with icy, cold water as you'll do a bit of bushwhacking and wading through soggy soil to find the most desirable shots. **Note**: This location is for the photographer who does not mind pushing through willows and sloshing through mud and water to find an acceptable composition.

Beaver pond on Schofield Pass Road. Taken at dawn, late July.

Cascades on Cascade Mountain

Cascades on Cascade Mountain - If you enjoy photographing waterfalls and cascades, you may want to visit this location; however, it will require a high-clearance vehicle. In late afternoon the waterfalls and cascades will be shaded by mountains. **Directions**: To reach this location from Crested Butte, take Gothic Road toward the ski resort. Turn left in about 2/3 mile on Slate River Road (Forest Road 734) and go approximately 7 miles. At the old mining town of Pittsburgh, turn left on Poverty Gulch Road. (You will have to drive through the river just after the turn.) Follow for about 2 miles; veer right at the fork. Drive another 100 yards or so and park on the side of the road. Do not drive this right fork very far as it comes to an abrupt halt where the road is completely washed out and dangerous to back up or turn around. Many of the falls and cascades are upstream and not visible from where you'll park. Hike uphill along the stream for several hundred yards to see additional cascades and falls. Depending on the year, you may also find ample wildflowers to photograph at this location.

San Juan Mountains

San Juan Mountains (Trails Illustrated Map 141) - The San Juan Mountains have long been recognized as an outstanding place to find breathtaking scenery and fields of magnificent summer wildflowers. Every year many tourists travel through the region in awe of the majestic mountains, but never witness the incredible array of brilliant wildflowers nestled in their basins. Some of my favorite San Juan Mountain locations that consistently yield productive shooting year after year are on the following pages.

Lower Falls in Yankee Boy Basin. Taken at dawn, early August.

Ouray, Colorado is called the "Switzerland of America." It's a charming summer tourist destination with surrounding areas offering spectacular wildflowers. Additionally, this town has large hot springs which are perfect for relaxing after a long day's shoot. Use the following website and phone number to help you make lodging/camping reservations:

www.ouraycolorado.com
Ouray Chamber of Commerce 800-228-1876

Map of San Juan Mountains

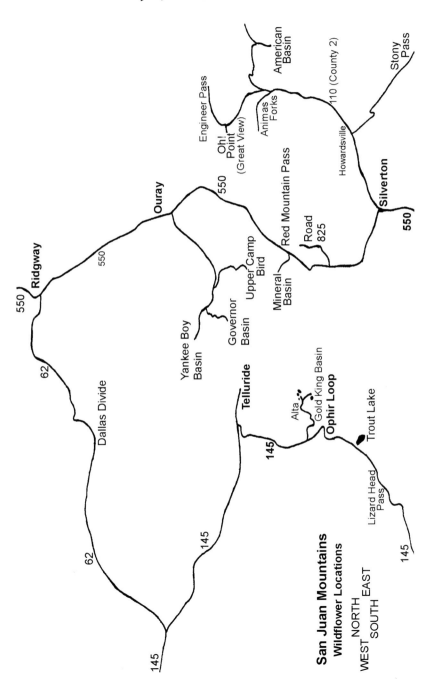

Yankee Boy Basin

Yankee Boy Basin - Without a doubt, this basin is the most famous wildflower location in Colorado. An immense variety of flowers may be found here. Often they are so thick that photographers find themselves surrounded by dizzying amounts of vibrant color. This set against an imposing background of dramatic mountains creates some of the greatest potential for wildflower and landscape photography in the Rockies. Much of this basin is privately owned, but fortunately, the mining company that owns the land allows photographers access provided they stay on trails and do not trample the vegetation. Please respect their wishes.

Photographers above timberline near the end of the road in Yankee Boy Basin. Scene shaded by clouds. Taken midday, late July.

Directions: From Ouray, drive south on U.S. Hwy 550. As you leave town and start winding up the mountain, make the first right turn on State Road 361 (also known as Forest Road 853 and Camp Bird Road). There may be signs for Box Canyon, Camp Bird and Sneffels. In a few hundred feet the road branches; keep left and follow State Road 361 (Forest Road 853) toward Camp Bird and Sneffels. In about 6.5 miles you'll reach the junction for Governor Basin (marked by a sign pointing toward Governor Basin). Follow the road to the right. Shortly after this junction, you will begin to see abundant wildflowers. Approximately 1/2 mile further, on your left, you will see several waterfalls; they are quite spectacular and frequently photographed. These waterfalls become shaded in late afternoon. From here the road continues to its end in another 1.5 miles. Flowers can be found throughout this basin, including along the trails above timberline.

The road into Yankee Boy Basin is well-maintained for the first few miles, but slowly and steadily deteriorates, eventually requiring a four-wheel drive. There are several precipitous portions along this road where you should use extreme caution.

People never cease to amaze me — just when you've determined something is impossible, somebody comes along to prove you wrong. The road into Yankee Boy Basin is quite rugged; some visitors park vehicles where it starts getting bumpy and walk. Some think the four-wheel drive road into the basin is almost effortless, while still others are terrified. One year we were taking a workshop into the basin and had traveled 1.5 miles locked in four-wheel drive. The road was very bumpy and only passable by high-clearance, four-wheel drive vehicles — or so I thought. As we rounded a bend, we saw an older, four-door sedan pulled to the side of the road. I was stupefied, as were the other passengers riding with me, to see a regular car that far up the basin, in one piece and seemingly without damage. How was it possible? I noticed the driver was still in his vehicle, so I rolled down my window to chat. As we approached, he got out, stretched, took in a deep breath of fresh mountain air and excitedly spoke in an Australian accent about how beautiful the surroundings were. Evidently he couldn't tell from our faces how impressed we were with his skillful driving, so I asked how he got his car this far in. He replied, "You know, it didn't seem so bad last night in the dark." With that we chuckled, shook our heads in disbelief and moved on.

Stony Pass

Stony Pass - Stony Pass is easily accessible by 4-wheel drive and usually has very good wildflower concentrations. Investigate both sides of this pass above tree line to make sure you don't miss any. For those who like to hike a little, park at the top of Stony Pass and hike west up the shoulder of Green Mountain to locate columbine and improve views of the surrounding landscape. **Directions**: Drive east out of Silverton on County Road 2; most maps also show this as Hwy 110 toward Howardsville. You'll reach Howardsville in approximately 4 miles where you will turn right (the only right turn available) on Forest Road 589. From this junction, it is approximately 7 miles to the top of Stony Pass and all of the turns along the way are well-marked.

Columbine on the shoulder of Green Mountain on west side of Stony Pass.

American Basin

American Basin - American Basin is a beautiful location to visit and one that is regularly photographed. You can 4-wheel directly into the heart of this dramatic location. Many flowers are present here, but I feel it is one of the best columbine hot spots in the state. **Directions**: Drive east out of Silverton on County Road 2; most maps also show this as Hwy 110. You'll travel through Eureka (about 7.5 miles from Silverton); in about 4 more miles, you'll approach Animas Forks. Veer right toward Engineer Pass, which will be marked by a sign. In about 1/2 mile, turn right toward Cinnamon Pass. Here the road becomes a little rougher and has precipitous sections; a four-wheel drive is recommended. Proceed up Cinnamon Pass and descend the other side. In less than 1/2 mile after descending to tree line, turn right on Forest Road 12 (expect to begin seeing flowers here) and follow to its end at a trailhead parking lot. Total distance to American Basin from Silverton is about 18 miles. Columbine may be abundant near the parking area and many more exhibited a short distance up the trail on the east flank of the basin above the trail.

Large fields of colombine can be found in American Basin.

The dirt roads that penetrate this part of the San Juans receive a lot of traffic. One time I came across two jeeps pulled to the side of the road, one with a flat tire. I asked the two couples if they were all right. They informed me they had it handled so I continued on to American Basin. Several hours later, on my return, I noticed the jeeps were still parked on the side of the road and their drivers were still struggling with the flat. I asked again if they needed any help. This time the answer was different, so I parked on the side of the road, and soon discovered the problem — they were trying to change a tire without any tools. Actually, they had the proper jack in one of the jeeps, but could not figure out how to remove it from its holder. Well, in a short time, we had overcome their dilemma, the tire change was nearing completion and one of their wives was starting to relax. She mentioned how in twenty years of four-wheeling they had never had a flat, but assumed their husbands could change one; after all, they were state troopers.

Gold King Basin

Gold King Basin - Gold King Basin is less frequently photographed, but a very rewarding location to visit. It has a variety of flowers with columbine and paintbrush usually the most plentiful. **Directions**: From Telluride, drive south on State Hwy 145 toward Ophir Loop. About 3 miles west of Telluride, there will be an intersection where Hwy 145 splits to the north and south. There's a gas station and a few other businesses at this intersection. Turn left, heading south, and follow about 5 miles until you see the Sunshine National Forest campground on the right and the road to Alta Lakes on the left. Turn left on Alta Lakes Road (Forest Road 623), marked by a road sign. Follow this road to the ghost town of Alta. You'll pass through its remains, cross the stream and continue uphill. At the next fork, turn right (unmarked) and follow this road to the small, unnamed lake that sits in Gold King Basin.

Sneezeweed in Gold King Basin

Wildflowers can be bountiful around this lake and further up the road, higher in the basin. On warm, dry years, when it's harder to find fresh, attractive wildflowers, check higher in this basin and you'll likely find some of the freshest, vibrant flowers available in the San Juan region. A four-wheel drive is recommended for reaching Gold King Basin.

It may be worthwhile to visit Alta Lakes while you're in the area. They're less than a mile from Gold King Basin and easy to locate; just eliminate the last right turn toward Gold King Basin. Instead, continue straight and you'll reach them in about 1/2 mile. Of the three, my favorite is the furthest (most westerly) one. It has the most wildflower potential.

Mineral Basin

Mineral Basin - Mineral Basin is another of the less photographed locations that can surprise visitors with thick fields of paintbrush, sneezeweed and numerous columbine. **Directions**: To reach Mineral Basin from Ouray, drive south on U.S. Hwy 550 to the top of Red Mountain Pass. On the south side of the pass, turn right (west) on Forest Road 823. This is the road to Black Bear Pass. A four-wheel drive is recommended. About 1 mile up the road, you should begin to see various wildflowers. I strongly advise that you do not proceed over and down the west side of Black Bear Pass into Telluride. The road becomes one-way, extremely narrow, winding and rough, requiring you to back up and pull forward several times just to make the hairpin turns high on the sheer rock face of the mountain. The west side is for very advanced, experienced off-road drivers only.

Photographer shooting flowers in Mineral Basin.
Taken early morning in late July.

Upper Camp Bird

Upper Camp Bird - Upper Camp Bird is an abandoned mining camp high in the mountains above Camp Bird. Bluebells are often the most common flower found here; however, as with most locations, a wide variety of other species is usually present. **Directions**: To reach this location from Ouray, drive south on U.S. Hwy 550. As you leave Ouray and start winding up the mountain, make the first right turn on State Road 361 (also known as Forest Road 853 and Camp Bird Road). There may be signs for Box Canyon, Camp Bird and Sneffels. In a few hundred feet the road branches; keep left and follow State Road 361 (Forest Road 853) toward Camp Bird and Sneffels. Drive about 5.5 miles (1 mile past the mining area called Camp Bird), then turn left on Forest Road 869. Follow this road for approximately 3 miles; as you approach timberline, you will start seeing flowers. Forest Road 869 is a challenging four-wheel drive road for the experienced driver only.

Photography Tip: If you're trying to photograph wildflowers through the day and it's partly cloudy, simply set up your shot and wait for a cloud to shade your subject. Use a warming filter and your results should be acceptable. To find out more about warming filters see page 134.

Other Scenic Shooting Locations of the San Juan Mountains

Dallas Divide

Dallas Divide

Dallas Divide - This location is one of the most photographed in all of Colorado. The dramatic mountains are usually the main subject of any composition and an old log fence is often placed in the foreground. Dallas Divide can be photographed at various times of the day, but I prefer to shoot here in early morning. **Directions**: Dallas Divide is located on a paved road (State Hwy 62) and very easy to find. From Ridgway, head west on State Hwy 62, drive uphill for about 8 miles. Near the top of the hill is a large parking area on the left (south side) and another smaller parking area at the top of the hill on the left (where the old log fence is located). Through Dallas Divide, the land on both sides of State Hwy 62 is private property; please respect the wishes and rights of the property owners.

Governor Basin

Governor Basin - Governor Basin is likely to have wildflowers, too, but this location is notorious for the photogenic Humbolt Mine and scenic mountain background. **Directions**: From Ouray, drive south on U.S. Hwy 550. As you leave Ouray and start winding up the mountain, make the first right turn on State Road 361 (also known as Forest Road 853 and Camp Bird Road). There may be signs for Box Canyon, Camp Bird and Sneffels. In a few hundred feet the road branches, keep left and follow State Road 361 (Forest Road 853) toward Camp Bird and Sneffels. In about 6.5 miles you'll arrive at the junction for Governor Basin. Veer left on Forest Road 853.1C; follow it for about 3 miles into Governor Basin. A four-wheel drive vehicle is required.

Humbolt Mine, high above timberline in Governor Basin. Taken midday, early August.

Top of Forest Road 825

Top of Forest Road 825 - This location is not widely known, but has an incredible panoramic view of mountains in the southwest section of the San Juans, many of which tower over 13,000 feet. This location is ideal for shooting with a panoramic camera. The best times are sunrise and early morning; however, under the right circumstances, sunsets can be spectacular. **Directions**: To reach this location from Silverton, drive north on U.S. Hwy 550 about 5 miles, turn right on Forest Road 825. Follow approximately 2.75 miles to its highest point, a short distance above timberline. Park your vehicle and look for the best vantage point to view the south and southwest. The condition of Forest Road 825 can vary. Sometimes two-wheel drive cars can reach this location; other times, a four-wheel drive is recommended.

Always drive carefully and slowly even if the road seems to be in good condition. You never know when a bad dip may be hidden in a shadow or just around the corner. I consider myself a careful driver; however, during one workshop I was reminded you can never be too careful. It was evening and we were driving Forest Road 825 at 15 miles per hour when a huge crevasse — OK, a large dip appeared. We lurched across as several hideous noises came from the undercarriage. We were all shook up, but I found no visible damage to the vehicle. I'd driven Forest Road 825 earlier in the week and found it smooth due to a recent grading. Unfortunately, during the previous night, a gully washer thundered through the mountains, removing sections of the road. Later in Ouray, I was dropping off passengers and as the front door was opened, a terrible metal grinding sound vibrated through the vehicle. The impact from crossing that dip had bent the frame and one of the doors was out of alignment.

Animas Forks

Animas Forks - Animas Forks is a relatively well-preserved, ghost mining town that you'll find interesting to explore and photograph. Two-wheel drive cars are almost always able to reach this location, but drive carefully as the road gets rougher past Eureka. **Directions**: From Silverton, drive east about 12 miles on County Road 2; most maps also show this as State Hwy 110.

Little Molas Lake

Little Molas Lake - This little lake is one of the few easily accessible evening shooting locations in the area. If the air is calm, you can get a good mountain reflection in the water. **Directions**: From Silverton, travel about 5.5 miles south on US Hwy 550; turn right (west) on Little Molas Lake Road. The lake is located in less than one mile on the left side of the road (see map on page 51).

Little Molas Lake

Shrine Pass

Another area that usually produces outstanding mountain wildflowers and can be reached with ease is Shrine Pass. This is a much smaller location than the two previously discussed regions. It is just one relatively level mountain pass; however, it is wide and there are miles of trails to explore. I think it's worth investigating, especially if you happen to be traveling on I-70. Numerous old tree stumps that often have wildflowers growing around them and sometimes on them can be found here, as well as vast fields of wildflowers. **Directions**: From Denver, head west on I-70. After you pass through Frisco, you will start to climb Vail Pass. Exit at the top of Vail Pass (exit 190); turn left and cross over I-70 heading in the direction of the rest area. Stay on this gravel road (Shrine Pass Road, accessible by all vehicles) for about 2 miles to the top of the pass and turn left into the parking area. The top of Shrine Pass may not be recognizable as a pass, so look for the parking area. Walk up the dirt road behind the parking area for about 100 yards; the trailhead will be on your left. For the best wildflowers, hike about 2 miles to the top of Shrine Ridge and go either way. If you veer right, look for the best concentrations of paintbrush and lupine amongst the trees that dot the meadow. The ridge also gives you breathtaking views of the surrounding mountains and may be a good place for you to practice shooting panoramic photographs.

Paintbrush in Shrine Pass

Shrine Pass - View from Shrine Ridge

Map of Shrine Pass

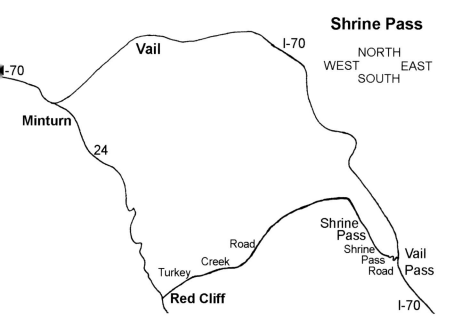

Autumn Foliage

Dallas Divide

Autumn Foliage

Autumn Foliage - The peak of Colorado's autumn foliage display varies with elevation and location. Higher elevations normally turn before lower elevations and different locations may peak at varying times. For most of Colorado, peak season usually occurs during the last two weeks of September or the first week of October. Usually the central mountain region of the state changes one week to ten days earlier than the southern mountains, including the San Juans.

Aspen leaves change to yellow, gold or sometimes fiery orange and provide the majority of color during autumn. When scrub oaks are present, they account for the remainder of color, adding various hues of orange and red to the landscape. Many mountain towns claim to have wonderful scenic drives to view fall colors; however, the locations described on the following pages are some of the premier hot spots for exceptional autumn shooting. Aspen forests are quite fickle, yielding peak colors for only a short duration and not necessarily at the same time as surrounding forests. If you do not find adequate color at one place, travel a few miles and you may discover a forest displaying peak color. If you are planning a driving trip over several days, it may be convenient to visit the locations as they're sequenced in this book.

The clouds part after a September snow storm to reveal portions of Maroon Bells.

Central Mountains

Map of Central Mountains

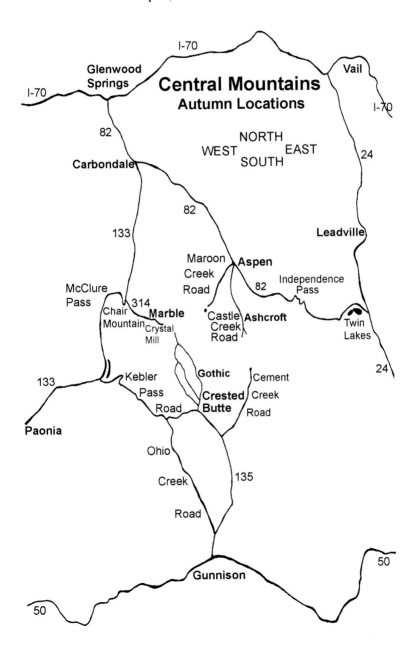

Aspen Area

Maroon Lake

Aspen, CO - With a name like Aspen, you'd expect this area to have lots of autumn color — and it does! My favorite location in the Aspen area is Maroon Lake, which is probably the most photographed and published lake in Colorado. Most photographs taken here place Maroon Lake in the foreground and the dramatic Maroon Bells in the background. This location photographs extremely well any time of the year, but due to large aspen stands, it is saturated with color during the autumn peak. The aspen here usually peak sometime during the last two weeks of September and before other locations in this guide. You'll want to photograph the lake during sunrise and early morning while the sun is behind you. Maroon Lake is just a few miles from Aspen and very easy to find. **Directions**: Drive north out of Aspen on State Hwy 82. As you leave town, but before you reach the airport, you will enter a traffic circle (roundabout). Take the Maroon Creek Road exit and follow about 10 miles to its end. Park in the large, paved parking lot. From the parking lot,

walk west on the trail about 100 yards to the lake. **Note**: In order to control the number of visitors June through September, Maroon Creek Road closes during the day from 8:30 a.m. to 5:00 p.m. During these times, a shuttle bus from Aspen transports visitors to the lake at a cost of $5.50 per person.

When visiting this area of Colorado, I often stay in Carbondale. It's centrally located so that you can reach Maroon Lake in about 45 minutes and the Chair Mountain and Marble area in about an hour. Use the following website and phone number to help you make hotel/camping reservations:

www.carbondale.com
Carbondale Chamber of
Commerce 970-963-1890

Maroon Bells and Maroon Lake near Aspen, CO.

Castle Creek Road

Another exceptional road for autumn colors in the Aspen area is Castle Creek Road. The first several miles of this road are in a tight valley with several homes. The valley eventually opens, revealing expansive views of aspen forest. About 10 miles up Castle Creek Road, you will find the ghost town of Ashcroft. For a $3.00 donation, you can walk in and shoot one of Colorado's most photogenic ghost towns with dramatic autumn colors in the background. I recommend traveling up Castle Creek Road as far as you can. Several miles past Ashcroft it will fork, both forks require 4-wheel drive. On foot or by vehicle, either of these roads can be rewarding.

Directions: To find Castle Creek Road, drive north out of Aspen on State Hwy 82. As you leave town, but before you reach the airport, you will enter a traffic circle (roundabout); take the Castle Creek Road exit.

Hotel in Ashcroft Ghost Town along Castle Creek Road.

Aspen forest along Castle Creek Road.

Marble

Marble (Trails Illustrated map 128) - Marble is a very small town nestled in the mountains with many colorful stands of aspen surrounding it. **Directions**: Take State Hwy 133 south out of Carbondale toward Redstone and Marble. As you approach the base of McClure Pass on Hwy 133, begin looking for shots. Turn left on Forest Road 314 (paved) and follow about 6 miles to the small town of Marble. Continue looking for shots along the way; there are many photographic opportunities along this drive. Marble is very small, but has several bed and breakfast establishments.

Horses and autumn color along Forest Road 314 between State Hwy 133 and Marble. Taken midmorning, late September.

Crystal Mill

Crystal Mill or Crystal Powerhouse, as some people refer to it, is located along a four-wheel drive road approximately 6 miles from Marble. This is another frequently photographed and published location. The rustic building sits on a rock face surrounded by aspen and above a rushing mountain river, however, the river's volume will have dramatically decreased by September. **Directions**: To reach Crystal Mill, stay on Forest Road 314 as it winds left and right through Marble.

As you leave Marble, you will pass Beaver Lake on the right; followed by a steep hill. At the top of the hill, veer right at the junction of the road to Lead King Basin. You'll pass a small lake (Lizard Lake) on your left. The road then curves left, heads downhill, becomes narrow, rough and has a steep drop on the right. For a few hundred yards, there is only enough room for one vehicle. If you have a passenger, you might want to send him/her to the bottom to hold traffic while you descend.

Note: Four-wheel driving rules require vehicles traveling downhill to back up and yield the right-of-way to vehicles traveling uphill. Be very careful through this section as some vehicles have lost control and dropped over the edge. At the bottom of the hill, the road becomes much easier. Drive about 2.75 miles further until you reach the large parking area for Crystal. The only building remaining is the mill, which is immediately across the river. The lighting is best here in the afternoon.

Note: Aspen trees in the Marble area often peak the same time as Maroon Lake aspen, usually during the third week of September.

Crystal Mill is the only location in the guide that doesn't really excite me. However, I've added it because it is a well-published location that many enjoy and continue to photograph.

Chair Mountain

Chair Mountain has large stands of aspen and is dramatic enough from several locations to be very photogenic, especially if capped by fresh snow. **Directions**: Chair Mountain is located directly west of the junction of Forest Road 314 and State Hwy 133. The eastern side photographs well near this intersection and the lighting on this side is best in the morning. To photograph the west side of Chair Mountain, drive State Hwy 133 over McClure Pass. After McClure Pass, 133 gradually curves to the south, revealing panoramic views of immense aspen forests, scrub oak and Chair Mountain, which is now to the east. Drive this area slowly, exploring side roads and turn-outs as you find them. This side of Chair Mountain is best photographed in the afternoon and evening. Further south on State Hwy 133 is the small town of Paonia, which offers several small motels and a few restaurants.

Chair Mountain along State Hwy 133, east of the junction with Forest Road 314. Taken midmorning, late September.

Crested Butte Area

Crested Butte (Trails Illustrated Map 133) - This town is a charming tourist destination surrounded by breathtaking mountain scenery. Aspen trees in this area usually peak after those in the vicinity of Maroon Lake and Marble. While many roads of the area will lead you through numerous stands of aspen, there are three roads which are particularly rewarding to drive.

Kebler Pass Road

Kebler Pass Road runs through the middle of an enormous aspen forest and is a well-maintained dirt road suitable for passenger cars. **Directions**: Kebler Pass Road (County Road 12) is the main road heading west out of Crested Butte. It eventually terminates at State Hwy 133; approximately 26 miles. Generally, the lighting is best at most locations along this road in the afternoon and early evening, however many locations will photograph quite well in the morning.

Near Kebler Pass Road
midmorning

Near Gothic Road
midmorning

Gothic Road

Gothic Road (Forest Road 317) - For over 7 miles, Gothic Road will take you past large stands of aspen that photograph well in the morning and afternoon. This road is well-maintained and passable by car. **Directions**: In Crested Butte, State Hwy 135 ends, but the road continues and is called Gothic Road. Drive it from the town of Crested Butte toward the ski resort, about 2 miles. Follow through the resort. As you leave the dense housing area, the road turns to dirt. In about 6 miles you'll reach the small settlement of Gothic.

Ohio Creek Road

Ohio Creek Road (County Road 730) is another road that winds through huge stands of aspen. Morning provides the best lighting at most locations along this road. If there has been a lot of snow, the road may be closed; otherwise it's reasonably well-maintained and usually passable by car. Campers and trucks may be restricted. **Directions**: Ohio Creek Road is reached by heading west out of Crested Butte on Kebler Pass Road (County Road 12). Near the top of Kebler Pass, about 6.25 miles, turn left (south) on Ohio Creek Road. There should be a road sign for Ohio Creek Road and/or Ohio Pass. Drive about 2.5 miles and you will find an immense aspen forest to enjoy as you wind down the south side of Ohio Pass.

San Juan Mountains

San Juan Mountain (Trails Illustrated Map 141) - The San Juan Mountains will never fail to leave an impression on the beholder. This is especially true during autumn when hues of yellow, orange and red play across the rugged terrain. Add deep blue skies and white snow-capped peaks to complete the ingredients of every landscape photographers' dreams. In this region, the foliage usually displays peak colors during the last week of September and the first week of October. Most of the area will satisfy your taste for autumn color; however, the following roads and locations are exceptionally superb.

View of Mount Sneffels at sunset near Dallas Creek Road.

The towns where you can expect to find lodging in this area are Ouray, Telluride and Ridgway. My personal favorite is Ouray, an old mining town nestled tightly in the mountains and very popular with tourists. Tourism dwindles in autumn and great lodging deals may be available. Telluride is an extremely popular ski resort town surrounded by breathtaking mountains. Ridgway is a small town with a few motels and serves more as a crossroads. Use the following websites and phone numbers to help you make hotel/camping reservations:

www.ridgwaycolorado.com   Ridgway Chamber of Commerce 800-220-4959
www.ouraycolorado.com   Ouray Chamber of Commerce   800-228-1876
www.visittelluride.com   Telluride Chamber of Commerce 888-605-2578

Map of San Juan Moumtains

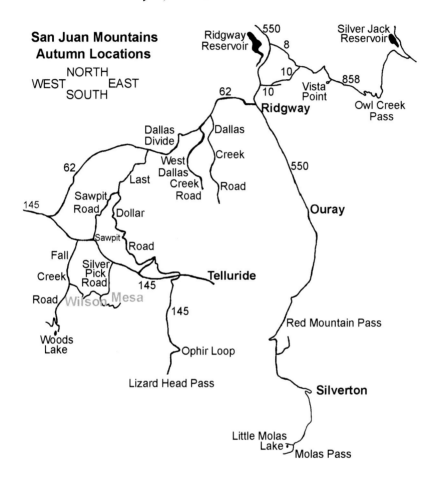

**San Juan Mountains
Autumn Locations**

NORTH
WEST   EAST
SOUTH

550

Ridgway
Reservoir

8

Silver Jack
Reservoir

10

62

10

858

Vista
Point

Ridgway

Owl Creek
Pass

Dallas
Divide

Dallas

Creek

62

West
Dallas
Creek
Road

550

Last

Road

Ouray

145

Sawpit
Road

Dollar

Sawpit

Road

Fall

Silver
Pick
Road

Telluride

145

Creek

Road

Wilson Mesa

145

Red Mountain Pass

Woods
Lake

Ophir Loop

Lizard Head Pass

Silverton

Little Molas
Lake

Molas Pass

Photography Tip: I shoot with Fuji Velvia, an outstanding landscape film providing sharp images with saturated colors. Velvia has a tendency to exaggerate the colors green and blue. This can be detrimental during autumn shooting because aspen leaves tend to appear yellow to the eye, but still have enough green left in them for Velvia to sense and exaggerate — your resulting image has green leaves. You can avoid this by shooting Kodak slide film that comes in a yellow and red box or use a color intensifier. The Singh-Ray color intensifier exaggerates warm colors (yellows, reds, oranges) and counters the greening tendency of Velvia film, producing realistic images.

Dallas Divide

Dallas Divide is scenic anytime of the year; however during autumn, it absolutely bursts with color. This location is plentiful with both aspen and scrub oak displaying a wide spectrum of colors against a backdrop of rugged, snow-capped peaks. I generally prefer shooting here during sunrise and early morning because it's when the lighting is best suited for the grand landscape scene that is available. However, Mt. Sneffels, one of Colorado's peaks exceeding 14,000 feet, is in this range and receives its best light in the late afternoon. **Directions**: Dallas Divide is conveniently located on a paved highway and very easy to find. From Ridgway, head west on State Hwy 62, travel uphill for over 8 miles. Near the top of the hill, there will be a large parking area on the left (south side) and another smaller parking area further up the hill on the left. Through Dallas Divide, the land on both sides of State Hwy 62 is private property. Please respect the wishes and rights of the property owners.

Dallas Divide

Dallas Creek Road & West Dallas Creek Road

Dallas Creek Road (also known as Forest Road 851 and County Road 7) and West Dallas Creek Road (also known as Forest Road 850 and County Road 9) are two roads in the Dallas Divide area that you really <u>must explore</u>, but be careful, as the views can be distracting. Both roads wind 6 to 7 miles through private property before reaching Uncompahgre National Forest; they end about one mile after the forest boundary. They are reasonably maintained with only a few rough spots, passable by most passenger cars. **Directions**: To find Dallas Creek Road from Ridgway, travel west about 4 miles on State Hwy 62; turn left on Dallas Creek Road. To find West Dallas Creek Road, travel another 1.25 miles further west on State Hwy 62 and turn left. **Note**: This turn may be hard to recognize because the fencing and gate style make it appear as though you're entering a private ranch.

Mt. Sneffels viewed from Dallas Creek Road

Last Dollar Road

Last Dollar Road (also known as Forest Road 638 and County Road 58P) - is one of my favorite drives, winding in and out of meadows, aspen forests and sometimes revealing spectacular views of Wilson Mesa and Wilson Peak. I prefer to photograph along this road during the morning; however, the afternoon offers opportunities as well. Most of this road is reasonably maintained and passable by car, but there may be a few spots that are too rough for a low-clearance vehicle. **Directions**: To find Last Dollar Road from Ridgway, head west on State Hwy 62. Shortly after passing the crest of Dallas Divide, turn left on Last Dollar Road (about 8.5 miles west of Ridgway). This road winds in and out of private property and national forest for over 21 miles and eventually connects with State Hwy 145, about 3 miles west of Telluride.

Corrals along Last Dollar Road

Wilson Mesa

Wilson Mesa is located near dramatic Wilson Peak. From the mesa, Wilson Peak photographs very well and has many aspen forests visible on its slopes. The lighting is best during sunrise and early morning. There are several roads on the mesa that deserve exploration, but the best and quickest access is Silver Pick Road (also known as Forest Road 622 and County Road 60M). **Directions**: From Ridgway, drive west on State Hwy 62; at the junction with State Hwy 145, turn left on Hwy 145, heading toward Telluride. (Watch carefully for this left turn as Hwy 62 does not have a stop sign here; the road continues straight and becomes Hwy 145.) After passing the small town of Sawpit, make the next right on Silver Pick Road (about 2.5 miles east of Sawpit). You may reach portions of Wilson Mesa by staying on Silver Pick Road and going all the way up to the mesa (about 4 miles) or you may choose to make the first right turn (unnamed) about 3.5 miles up Silver Pick Road. Both directions will take you to the top of the mesa and into view of Wilson Peak and aspen forests.

Photograph of Wilson Peak and Wilson Mesa captured from Last Dollar Road.

State Highway 145

State Highway 145 between Telluride and Lizard Head Pass offers views of many large aspen forests and is well worth your time. Lizard Head Pass has breathtaking views, but they don't seem to photograph as well as they appear to the eye. I think the light for shooting along this route is best in the morning.

Photography Tip: Deep blue sky and rich golden leaves create an attractive contrast. A polarizing filter is often useful to maximize this effect. To find out more about a polarizing filter see page 128.

Owl Creek Pass

Owl Creek Pass is accessed by Forest Road 858 and is approximately 10 miles east of U.S. Hwy 550. Forest Road 858 travels through more than 18 miles of aspen forest and meadows. As you drive up the pass, be sure to explore Vista Point, an overlook that offers a scenic view of large aspen forests and Courthouse Mountain. There should be a sign where you turn right toward Vista Point. Forest Road 858 is reasonably maintained and passable by car; however, there may be a few rough spots requiring special attention. Many enjoy taking this road completely over the pass to Silver Jack Reservoir and down to Hwy 50. You can also approch this pass from Highway 50 by turning south on Cimarron road just east of Cimarron. This may be a productive route to take if you're approaching the San Juans from Crested Butte. **Directions**: To find Owl Creek Pass from Ridgway, drive north on U.S. Hwy 550. Turn right on County Road 10; follow about 3 miles and turn right on County Road 8, which eventually becomes Forest Road 858.

Aspen stand on west side of Owl Creek Pass.

Photography Tip: Do you long for images with the color saturation found in magazines? Use slide film. From my experience, most Kodak and Fuji slide films have superior color saturation over print films. Additionally, with slide film, what you do with the camera is the only thing that affects the outcome of your images. Unlike print film, the processor plays no role in manipulating color balance or exposure. This makes slide film the best choice for those learning photography because mistakes will not be corrected by the processor. During one of our workshops, we were shooting on a gray, overcast day. Later, when viewing the images that one of the participants had taken with print film, we were amazed to see blue sky. The processor simply decided blue sky was desirable and created it in the prints.

Red Mountain Pass

U.S. Hwy 550 from Montrose to Durango will take you in and out of some very beautifully photogenic autumn scenery. I recommend driving the entire route to find where the colors are peaking and the scenery that best suits your taste. One of my favorite stretches of 550 is between Ouray and Red Mountain Pass. This stretch of road has numerous stands of aspen and several photogenic old mines along the east side of the road. The afternoon usually produces the best lighting for photographing the mines. **Directions**: To find the top of Red Mountain Pass from Ouray, drive about 10 miles south on U.S. Hwy 550. Drive slowly so as not to miss the generous scenery or the extremely steep cliffs.

A neat little ghost town with several well-preserved homes is **Ironton**, located just off U.S. Hwy 550, north of Red Mountain Pass. It may not be the most photogenic location, but if you're interested in ghost towns, it's certainly worth a visit. **Directions**: As you head up Red Mountain Pass from Ouray, you'll climb a steep, narrow canyon. In approximately 5 or 6 miles the road levels in a large valley; Crystal Lake will be on the right. From this point, travel about 2 more miles and turn left onto County Road 20D, a small, tree-lined, dirt road. Ironton is located just a few hundred feet down this road.

One of the old mines along Hwy 550 in Red Mountain Pass

Old mine located on Red Mountain Pass. This image was photographed on a hazy, partly overcast day. While the San Juans are great for autumn images, they're also my favorite mountains for shooting winter landscapes. March is usually the best month to capture winter in Colorado. Taken midafternoon, March.

Woods Lake

Woods Lake - I'm often asked where the best late afternoon shooting locations are. Well, if there is snow on the mountains and the aspen are near their peak, you should try shooting at Woods Lake. This lake does not look like much to the eye, as it has a lot of aquatic plant life compared with most Colorado lakes, but it does photograph well. To get the best lighting for the aspen and the lake, you need to be shooting in advance of sunset, so be there in late afternoon to scout locations. I usually shoot from the dam and use a jacket to cover a potentially annoying sign in the composition on the far shore. **Directions**: From Telluride, take State Hwy 145 west for about 13 miles. Shortly past Sawpit, make a left hand turn on Forest Road 618 and follow for about 9 miles to the lake.

Woods Lake, late afternoon

Little Molas Lake

Little Molas Lake - It does not have a lot of aspen, but it is still a good evening shooting location. If the air is calm, you can get a good mountain reflection in the water. **Directions**: From Silverton, travel about 5.5 miles south on US Hwy 550; turn right (west) on Little Molas Lake Road. The lake is located in less than one mile on the left side of the road.

Little Molas Lake, late afternoon

State Highway 149

State Hwy 149 between Lake City and Slumgullion Pass has many large stands of aspen and turnouts for viewing them. Some of these locations allow you to create compositions with mountains in the background. This stretch of road is usually best to photograph in the morning. By the afternoon, you'll be shooting into the sun in order to include mountains in your composition. **Directions**: From Lake City, head south on State Hwy 149. A few miles out of town you will start gaining elevation and views of aspen that are worth shooting. The best shooting is over by the time you reach the top of Slumgullion Pass. While you're in this vicinity, you may wish to also investigate **North Clear Creek Falls** (see map below).

Map of Highway 149

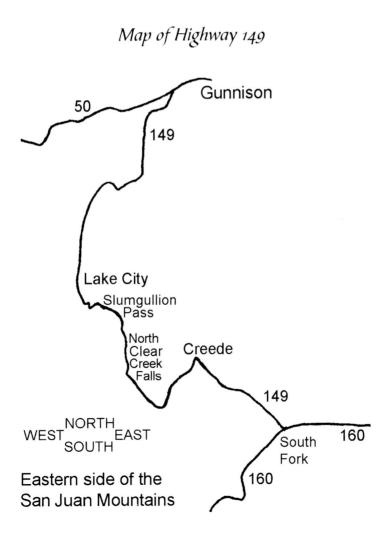

Rocky Mountai

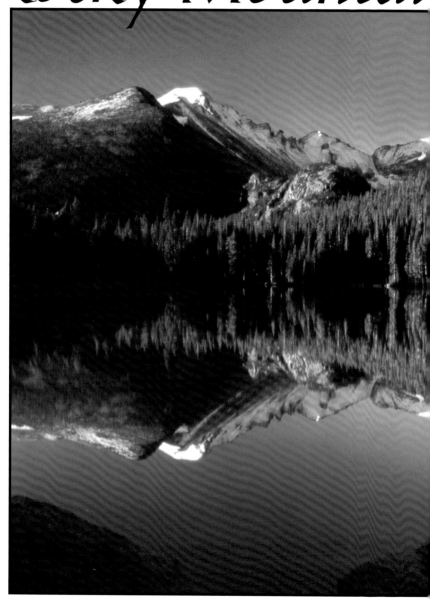

National Park

Bear Lake

Rocky Mountain National Park

Rocky Mountain National Park (Trails Illustrated Map 200) - Many visitors to Colorado, including serious photographers, spend time in Rocky Mountain National Park (RMNP). The park isn't known for abundant wildflowers or fall colors; however, it does have spectacular scenic views with mountain lakes and streams, bounteous wildlife, and the opportunity to drive above timberline on a paved road. Trail Ridge Road, known for its amazing vistas and breathtaking beauty at every turn, offers endless photographic opportunities of the region's dramatic mountains. Many visitors to the Rockies are not acclimated to the elevation and easily tire with minimal exertion. Although I will discuss a few longer hikes, most of the shooting locations mentioned require little physical effort to reach.

Wondering where to stay when visiting Rocky Mountain National Park? Estes Park is the town situated at the east entrance to RMNP. Grand Lake, a much smaller town, is at the west entrance. Both are charming; however, Estes Park is considerably closer to most of the shooting locations described in this guide. Use the following website and phone number to help you make hotel/camping reservations:

www.EstesParkResort.com
Estes Park Chamber Resort Association (970) 586-4431

Golden-Mantled Ground Squirrel

Rocky Mountain National Park Map

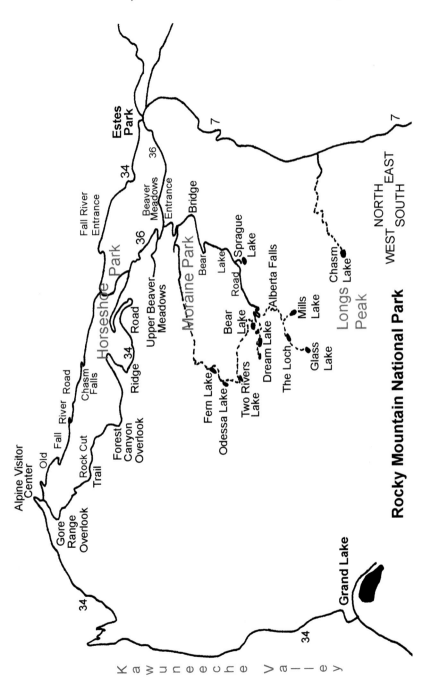

Sprague Lake

Sprague Lake is easy to find and requires only a stroll across level ground to photograph. Many published images of RMNP are taken here. The image most often captured positions the lake in the foreground with a background of majestic, snow-capped mountains; many also include a small rock poking out of the water on the east side of the lake. Dawn is usually the best time to shoot here. As the sun rises over the eastern plains, the towering mountains of the park seize the day's first light and display a pinkish glow called "alpen glow". **Directions**: To find Sprague Lake from Estes Park, enter RMNP at the Beaver Meadows Entrance, take the first left turn, Bear Lake Road, and drive approximately 6 miles. At the sign to Sprague Lake, turn left and follow this road about 1/3 mile to the parking lot. Follow the trail approximately 70 yards to the lake; proceed in either direction around the lake to the opposite side (about a 10-minute walk), where you'll find a small bridge crossing the stream that flows out of the lake.

Sprague Lake, midmorning

Time and again, I've set up to photograph at Sprague Lake only to turn around and find an astonishing shot in the opposite direction. The lesson: Try to anticipate your shot, but continuously absorb the surroundings for other possibilities, especially at sunrise and sunset.

It's very common to see wildlife in Rocky Mountain National Park. One June day a friend and I were photographing sunset at Sprague Lake and were amazed to see an elk standing in the water; they don't normally wade waist deep into lakes. We happened to be walking along a trail which led us near its position. Since elk are common in the park, close encounters are frequent so we paid little attention to our proximity. When we reached the point where there was no vegetation between us and the animal, our new, uncomfortably close viewing revealed it was in fact a bull moose.

He stopped chewing and stared at us in a manner that suggested we keep moving. We were eager to oblige. You do not want to crowd a moose; they are unpredictable and can be very aggressive. When annoyed, they may kick, stomp, and trample you. We were extremely surprised to see a moose here as they typically inhabit the Kawuneeche Valley on the western side of the park.

The Big Thompson River

The Big Thompson River, as it flows through the park, can be very photogenic. In June, while the river is swollen with snow melt, it offers great shooting as it energetically cascades over large boulders. This is found near the southeast corner of Moraine Park where the Big Thompson flows into the woods and under Bear Lake Road. Photograph from the bridge that Bear Lake Road uses to cross the river. During the month of June, at approximately 10:30 a.m., the shadow of the bridge will move out of the way, creating an opportunity for an impressive image.

Directions: To find this location from Estes Park, enter RMNP at the Beaver Meadows Entrance; take the first left turn, Bear Lake Road, and drive approximately 2.5 miles to the bridge.

Big Thompson River cascade in Rocky Mountain National Park. Taken from the bridge about 11:00 a.m. in early June.

In **Moraine Park**, the Big Thompson takes on the characteristics of a mature river twisting and turning as it slowly winds through this enormous meadow. Many breathtaking images have been captured here at various times of the year; photographs well in the morning and in evening if clouds are present. **Directions**: To find Moraine Park from Estes Park, enter RMNP at the Beaver Meadows Entrance; take the first left turn, Bear Lake Road, and drive approximately 1.25 miles to Moraine Park, a gigantic meadow stretching 3/4 mile wide and almost 2 miles long. You may turn right toward Fern Lake Trailhead, park where it interests you and wander along the river. However, I usually stay on Bear Lake Road as it crosses Moraine Park and just before it leaves the meadow (about 0.4 mile), turn right on a short road leading to a small dirt parking lot, used mainly by fishermen. From here, walk west along the river seeking a variety of compositions that include the river.

Big Thompson River in Moraine Park. Taken at sunset, June.

Longs Peak

Longs Peak dominates much of the landscape and is the park's only mountain exceeding 14,000 feet in elevation. During spring and summer, while aspens have their leaves, I like to photograph Longs Peak from the parking lot at Upper Beaver Meadows trailhead. From this location, you can use two large aspen trees to frame Longs Peak. **Directions**: To find this parking lot from Estes Park, enter RMNP at the Beaver Meadows Entrance; stay on U.S. Hwy 36 for a little over 2 miles, then turn left on the dirt road to Upper Beaver Meadows. Follow until it ends at the trailhead parking lot (about 1.5 miles). The two aspens are found along the brook on the south edge of the parking lot.

Longs Peak from Upper Beaver Meadow.
Taken late morning in June.

Chasm Falls

If you wish to see as much of the park as possible from your car, consider **Old Fall River Road**. It's a well-maintained, one-way, dirt road that takes you above

timberline to the Alpine Visitor Center (9 miles). **Note:** The Visitor Center closes at 4:00 p.m. **Chasm Falls** is located along this road and is well worth seeing and photographing. Because I prefer to shoot waterfalls in the shade, I travel this road in the late afternoon. As you leave timberline, search the high alpine valleys and hillsides carefully; many deer and elk inhabit this area during late spring, summer and early autumn. By embarking in the late afternoon, you'll arrive at Trail Ridge Road a short time before sunset, which can be very rewarding to photograph from. **Directions**: To find Old Fall River Road from Estes Park, enter RMNP at the Fall River Entrance; about 2.25 miles past the entrance, turn right on the paved road. In approximately 2 miles, the road becomes Old Fall River Road.

Chasm Falls, Taken late afternoon in August.

Trail Ridge Road

Gore Range Overlook is located above timberline and is a spectacular location for large-scale mountain scenes during sunrise and sunset. A panoramic camera can be very useful here. One of the key ingredients for exceptional shots at this overlook is clouds; their glow with sunrise or sunset light will create breathtaking images.

Another nearby overlook worth exploring is **Forest Canyon Overlook**. This location often photographs best during sunrise. Even during summer, it can be very cold and windy in the morning above timberline, so bring your winter jacket, hat and gloves. **Directions**: From Estes Park, enter RMNP at either entrance and proceed along U.S. Hwy 34 or U.S. Hwy 36 until they intersect.

At their junction, take Trail Ridge Road (U.S. Hwy 34) west toward Grand Lake and proceed approximately 11.5 miles; turn left into the Forest Canyon Overlook parking lot. The Gore Range Overlook is another 5.5 miles further west on Trail Ridge Road, also a left-hand turn into the parking lot.

Trail Ridge Road; photographer near Rock Cut Trail parking lot.

Never rush a location. One August during monsoon season, we had our workshop group get up extra early so we could reach the Gore Range Overlook for dawn. Because of excess moisture resulting from monsoon season, we were expecting to find clouds below our position and mountain tops above. Upon arrival there were no clouds below, disappointment set in and the group was disheartened. However, we sat and waited. Much to our delight, over the next ten minutes, a large bank of clouds developed exactly where we wanted. They wrapped the lower elevations of the high mountains in a fluffy, white blanket while the rugged mountain tops were visible above.

Bear Lake

Bear Lake is the most popular destination and has the largest parking lot in Rocky Mountain National Park. Mornings, during summer, this parking lot fills to capacity; then shuttle buses transport people to and from the lake. Don't let this discourage you from shooting Bear Lake as breathtaking scenery awaits. I advise photographing here at dawn; the lighting is best and you'll avoid crowds. **Note:** Park rangers will ticket cars parked overnight without a permit. If you're planning on arriving several hours before dawn and leaving your car in the parking lot, you should leave a note on your windshield informing park rangers that you haven't parked overnight.

Directions: To reach Bear Lake from Estes Park, enter RMNP at the Beaver Meadows Entrance; make the first left turn on Bear Lake Road. Continue on this winding, mountain road until it ends in the Bear Lake parking lot (about 9 miles). The lake is located about 100 yards from the parking lot and has a well-worn trail around it.

The toughest decision is usually where to shoot when the light hits. The east shore of Bear Lake provides several interesting shots capturing Hallett Peak reflecting in water, while the north shore offers spectacular views of Longs Peak. If you scout your positions in advance and move quickly, you may be able to shoot both during sunrise. If you're going to try this, I recommend shooting Longs Peak from the north shore first. At sunset, if the clouds are suitable and glowing with color, Bear Lake's north shore can offer delightful images of Longs Peak. For those who wish to do a little hiking, even more captivating scenery awaits a short distance up the trail at Dream Lake. This hike requires moderate physical exertion.

Longs Peak reflecting in Bear Lake during sunrise. This image was photographed from the north shore of Bear Lake facing south toward Longs Peak. Taken at sunrise, August.

An exciting encounter with elk happened at Bear Lake. It was dawn and we had a workshop group on the edge of the lake photographing sunrise. When we arrived, there were no animals present, but after cameras were positioned, about ten elk drifted out of the forest to the lake's edge, intermingling with our group. Dawn at Bear Lake is usually worth the early rise, but having elk up close was definitely an added thrill.

Nymph Lake; Dream Lake; Emerald Lake

Nymph Lake, only 3/4 mile from Bear Lake, is a smaller lake passed on the way to Dream Lake. Consider shooting it from the high rocks on its north side where you'll be able to include Longs Peak in the composition. This location can produce great early morning shots, however exercise caution when climbing on the rocks.

A little further up the trail, about 1/3 mile, is **Dream Lake**. Dream Lake is very photogenic; it can blow your mind and rolls of film at sunrise. Hallett Peak will be close and stunning in dawn's magical light. If you miss dawn, don't despair; this lake is a gem for most of the morning. You may need a wide-angle lens, 28 mm or wider, to do the lake justice. Most photographs are taken from the east shore near where the trail meets the lake.

Nymph Lake and Longs Peak shrouded in clouds. Photographed from rocks above the north shore of the lake. Taken at sunrise, August.

Dream Lake photographed from the east shore facing west toward Hallett Peak. Taken midmorning, June.

The next lake up this trail is **Emerald Lake**, about 3/4 mile; it's beautiful, but not nearly as photogenic as Dream Lake. It is so close to the mountains that a 20 mm or wider is required to gather all of the scenery. If you enjoy hiking, you may find the hike on to Emerald Lake worthwhile.

Photography Tip: Use a color intensifier when shooting sunrises and sunsets to maximize the color saturation of the pinks, reds and yellows often available during these times. To find out more about intensifiers, see page 133.

Alberta Falls

Alberta Falls is a popular, short hiking destination that photographs well early in the morning or late in the day. After photographing Alberta Falls, consider hiking upstream where you may find unique and interesting compositions along the water. **Directions**: From Estes Park, enter RMNP at the Beaver Meadows Entrance; make the first left on Bear Lake Road. On a sharp, right curve near the end of Bear Lake Road (about 8.5 miles) is the small parking lot for the Glacier Gorge Junction

Trailhead. Park and proceed across the road and up the trail to Alberta Falls, about 1/2 mile hike. There are lots of aspen along the trail making it a good choice during autumn. **Note**: This parking lot usually fills to capacity by 7:30 a.m.

Albert Falls, early morning

Photography Tip: Maximum depth of field is obtained by using the smallest aperture setting (largest number) available, but where do you focus? With landscapes, focusing on your foreground subject will usually produce the sharpness desired throughout the image.

Wildlife

Many people visit national parks to see wildlife. Rocky Mountain National Park is certainly no exception. Fortunately, it has enough wildlife to delight every visitor. By far the most common and readily found large animal is **elk**. This majestic creature inhabits almost every corner of the park, but some locations consistently deliver sightings. Elk are in Moraine Park practically every morning and evening of the year. During the fall rut, one of the best places to view them is from the rocks on the west side of Moraine Park, about 300 yards down the Cub Lake Trail.

Elk are also regularly found in Horseshoe Park. During spring and mid-autumn, it's not uncommon to find elk nonchalantly standing in and strolling through the town of Estes Park. After the snow melts in the spring and before it flies again in autumn, one of the most promising locations to find and photograph elk is above timberline. Simply drive up Trail Ridge Road until you spot them. The Kawuneeche Valley, located on the west side of the park, north of Grand Lake, is another hot spot for elk.

This valley is also one of the most likely places for finding **moose**. Moose are rare in Colorado and it's a real treat to observe them. **Big horn sheep** are also rare in Colorado, but may be found in the park. They frequently venture down to mineral deposits in the vast meadow just inside the Fall River Entrance at the east end of Horseshoe Park. **Golden-mantled ground squirrels** are adorable little creatures and quite photogenic. I doubt any park visitor has been able to nibble a snack or rest for a period of time without making the acquaintance of the park's most gifted panhandler. Years of skillful interaction has made humans very approachable by this clever little rodent. Photographing them should be easy at most locations, but please don't feed them.

Bull elk and cows in Moraine Park. Typically you can observe rutting behavior from the second week of September through the first week of October. Taken early morning in September.

Trails of Rocky Mountain National Park to hike and photograph

One of the best ways to truly appreciate the magic that this national park has to offer is to park your car and enjoy some hiking. The tremendous beauty of the park becomes even more apparent when you reach its remote, hidden locations. Many of the park trails climb into unimaginable beauty where small lakes nestled in the bosom of the Rockies offer spectacular photographic opportunities. The following hikes are lengthy, requiring sustained exertion.

The Loch; Glass Lake; Mills Lake

The Glacier Gorge Junction parking lot is the starting point of hikes to several magnificent lakes. **The Loch** (2.25 miles), **Glass Lake** (3.25 miles), and **Mills Lake** (2 miles) are incredibly beautiful and photogenic. If you're a hiking photographer, you should not miss them. It's hard to select the best time of day because clouds and lighting can fire up at sunrise or sunset, splashing impressive color across the landscape. Don't forget to bring a detailed, topographic map of the area. **Directions**: To access Glacier Gorge Junction parking lot from Estes Park, enter RMNP at the Beaver Meadows Entrance; make the first left on Bear Lake Road. On a sharp, right curve near the end of Bear Lake Road (about 8.5 miles) is the small parking lot for the Glacier Gorge Junction Trailhead. Park and proceed across the road and up the trail to the lakes. **Note**: This parking lot usually fills to capacity by 7:30 a.m.

Glass Lake photographed from the rocks above it facing north-east. These rocks are located between Glass Lake and Sky Pond, near the shore of Sky Pond. Taken at sunrise, August.

Photograph of The Loch. Taken midday, August.

Chasm Lake

Chasm Lake is located on the east shoulder of Longs Peak and requires substantial physical effort to reach; elevation gain of 2,400 feet in 3.75 miles. This lake is a popular destination for serious hiking photographers. At sunrise, the east face of Longs Peak reflects warm, morning light in Chasm Lake. Don't forget to bring a detailed, topographic map of the area and plenty of water. The air in Colorado is very dry, requiring hikers to consume a large quantity of water in order to maintain proper hydration. Hydration and hiking strength go hand-in-hand; the more you drink, the stronger you hike. **Directions**: To find this lake from Estes Park, drive about 9.5 miles south on State Hwy 7 from U.S. Hwy 36; turn right on the road to East Longs Peak Trailhead. Hike Longs Peak trail above timberline about 3 miles to the marked junction with the trail to Chasm Lake. Note: When the trail to the top of Longs Peak is clear of snow, the trailhead parking lot can fill to capacity before 3:30 a.m. This usually happens during August and early September.

Fern Lake Trail

Fern Lake, **Odessa Lake** and **Two Rivers Lake** are astonishingly beautiful lakes that photograph well at dawn; to reach them this early will require you to start hiking a few hours before sunrise. Both Fern Lake and Odessa Lake are easy to find as the trail takes you directly to their shores. The last 100 yards on the approach to Odessa Lake is an extremely photogenic stretch of Fern Creek. Two Rivers Lake is a little more difficult to find because the trail does not take you directly to it. To locate it, pay attention to your detailed, topographic map and watch for it glistening through the trees. All three lakes are located along Fern Lake Trail which has two starting points. One is at Bear Lake: Two Rivers Lake, 2.75 miles; Odessa Lake, 3.75 miles; Fern Lake, 4.5 miles. The other is the Fern Lake Trailhead on the west end of Moraine Park: Fern Lake, 3.5 miles; Odessa Lake, 4.25 miles; Two Rivers Lake, 5.25 miles.

Two Rivers Lake photographed from its east shore facing west. Taken midday, September.

Odessa Lake. Taken at midmorning, September.
You'll find a 24 mm lens or wider useful here.

Fern Creek about 100 yards downstream of
Odessa Lake. Taken at sunrise, September.

Spring Photogr

phy

Dream Lake, Rocky Mountain National Park

Spring Photography

Spring Photography - Springtime in Colorado is an exhilarating experience. It provides breathtaking scenes of formidable, snow-capped peaks high in the background, while the foreground is filled with lush greens and a sprinkling of wildflowers. The vibrant green of new aspen leaves contrast well with the deep greens of pines, spruce and firs. This is a frequently overlooked shooting season, which is unfortunate, because you will find yourself photographing from lower elevations with less hiking and 4-wheel driving required. Actually, spring is one time where much of the state is far more photogenic as a result of the snow pack. Mountains that usually seem rounded or flat and dull appear dramatic and interesting with fields of snow creating contrast against rocky slopes. Additionally, you'll find streams and waterfalls are swollen, creating potential that does not exist later in the year. Usually this photography season starts sometime during the last two weeks of May. This is when the lower elevations in the approximate range of 8,000 to 9,000 feet begin to green. Usually by mid or late June, this season ends, as the foliage near timberline greens and alpine lakes thaw. There are several locations that will maximize your use of time for shooting this season. The following locations are offered not as an exclusive list, but to give you scenery-rich regions to start with. You will undoubtedly find more to photograph as you travel to these locations.

Dallas Divide

Dallas Divide - It is a truly wondrous experience to drive the back roads of this area in the spring. Many wildflowers are blooming, deer and elk are numerous, and great photographs can be produced in the morning and afternoon. Dallas Divide is just shy of 9,000 feet, so usually the last week of May is a suitable time to photograph here. Dallas Creek Road (also known as Forest Road 851 and County Road 7) and West Dallas Creek Road (also known as Forest Road 850 and County Road 9) are the two most interesting roads to explore, but be careful, the views can be distracting. Both roads wind 6 to 7 miles through private property before reaching Uncompahgre National Forest and then end about one mile after the forest boundary. They are reasonably maintained with only a few rough spots, passable by most passenger cars. **Directions**: To find Dallas Creek Road from Ridgway, travel west about 4 miles on State Hwy 62; turn left on Dallas Creek Road. To find West Dallas Creek Road, travel another 1.25 miles further west on State Hwy 62 and turn left. **Note**: This turn may be hard to recognize because the fencing and gate style make it appear as if you're entering a private ranch.

Dallas Divide - Dallas Creek Road

Maroon Lake

Maroon Lake - This is a favorite photography location any time of the year. It is especially dramatic in the spring when there is a lot of snow pack on Maroon Bells, the two peaks exceeding 14,000 feet that tower over the lake. The best lighting for this location is during sunrise and the first several hours of the day. There are trails in the area worth exploring and the roadside of Maroon Creek Road on the way to Maroon Lake can yield productive shooting. The elevation of Maroon Lake is just above 9,500 feet. Often the first part of June is a good time to photograph here. **Directions**: Drive north out of Aspen on State Hwy 82. As you leave town, but before you reach the airport, you will enter a traffic circle (roundabout). Take the Maroon Creek Road exit and follow about 10 miles to its end. Park in the large paved parking lot. From the parking lot, walk west on the trail about 100 yards to the lake. **Note**: In order to control the number of visitors June through September, Maroon Creek Road closes during the day from 8:30 a.m. to 5:00 p.m. During these times, a shuttle bus from Aspen transports visitors to the lake at a cost of $5.50 per person.

Maroon Bells reflecting in Maroon Lake

Rocky Mountain National Park

Because of the wide variety of elevations, there is always something to shoot in this park throughout the spring season. Please refer to page 63-77 for locations in Rocky Mountain National Park.

Photography Tip: Often the use of a one-stop split-neutral density filter is required during the spring to keep detail in the mountaintops and the sky from burning out (over-exposed). Learn more about these filters on page 128.

*Rocky Mountain National Park -
Nymph Lake and Longs Peak.*

Scenic Location.

Ashcroftt (Ghost Town)

Colorado's Scenic Locations

Virtually all of Colorado is breathtaking to behold; its mountainous regions particularly stunning, causing it to be an extremely popular vacation destination. Even so, there are certain locations that are photographed far more frequently than others.

Every time I've returned from Wyoming to Colorado, driving south on State Hwy 125, I am invariably impressed with the scenic beauty that surrounds the North Park region near Walden. However, this region is not a common destination for photographers. Why? Because it does not yield a lot of calendar-quality images. Photographers are like fishermen. Fishermen go where there are big fish and lots of them; photographers go where there is incredible photogenic scenery and lots of it. The scenic locations mentioned in this section are certainly not the only ones; rather they are a selection of some of the most popular with an abundance of photogenic potential.

Medicine Bow Mountains east of Walden, Colorado. Taken at sunrise, February.

Maroon Bells & Maroon Lake

Maroon Bells & Maroon Lake define Colorado (Trails Illustrated Map 128). They must surely be the most published, rugged mountains and mountain lake scene of Colorado. Most photographs taken here place Maroon Lake in the foreground and the dramatic Maroon Bells in the background. This location photographs extremely well anytime of the year, however, the best lighting is found during sunrise and early morning while the sun is behind you. Maroon Lake is just a few miles from Aspen and very easy to find. **Directions**: Drive north out of Aspen on State Hwy 82. As you leave town, but before you reach the airport, you will enter a traffic circle (roundabout). Take the Maroon Creek Road exit and follow about 10 miles to its end. Park in the large, paved parking lot. From the parking lot, walk west on the trail about 100 yards to the lake.

Note: In order to control the number of visitors June through September, Maroon Creek Road closes during the day from 8:30 a.m. to 5:00 p.m. During these times, a shuttle bus from Aspen transports visitors to the lake at a cost of $5.50 per person.

Maroon Bells reflecting in Maroon Lake. Taken at dawn.

Dallas Divide

Dallas Divide - This location is one of the most photographed in all of Colorado. The dramatic mountains are usually the main subject of any composition. It can be photographed at various times of the day, but I prefer early morning. Dallas Divide is located on a paved road, State Hwy 62, and very easy to find. **Directions**: From Ridgway, drive west on State Hwy 62, uphill for about 8 miles. Near the top of the hill is a large parking lot on the left (south side) and another smaller parking area at the top of the hill, also on the left. Through Dallas Divide, the land on both sides of State Hwy 62 is private property. Please respect the wishes and rights of the property owners. See the map page 51.

Dallas Divide

The San Juan Mountains around Dallas Divide are loaded with photographic potential. For additional details, see the wildflower and autumn sections of this guide.

Sunrise from the top of Mount Evans

Mount Evans

Mount Evans is a spectacular and easily accessible location. A paved road winds past mountain lakes and ancient bristle cone pines to the top of this lofty mountain. With an elevation of 14,264 feet, Mount Evans is one of only 54 mountains in Colorado to tower above 14,000 feet. Both morning and late afternoon can produce suitable lighting, depending upon where you are on the mountain. My favorite time to photograph here is sunrise from the top. This is also one of the few times when you'll likely have the mountain to yourself, except for the mountain goats, which you will find in astonishing places.

The entrance to Mt Evans is open all night and has a self-pay station (current cost is $10.00). From the station, it should take about 30 minutes to reach the summit. There is plenty to photograph along the road to the top. Be sure to take advantage of the shooting from both Echo Lake and Summit Lake along the way. Also, as you approach timberline, look for a log structure and parking lot on the left side of the road. Here you will find a trailhead that provides access to ancient bristle cone pines whose twisted, grainy wood can make interesting photographs. Additionally, the mountain goats inhabiting the top of Mount Evans are surprisingly easy to approach and make excellent photographic subjects.

Directions: From Denver, drive west on I-70; use exit 240 (Mt Evans exit) and head south on State Hwy 103 approximately 16 miles. Turn right on State Hwy 5 and follow approximately 14 miles to the top of Mount Evans. **Note**: Hwy 5 is usually only open Memorial Day to Labor Day.

Echo Lake, midmorning

Map of the Mount Evans Area

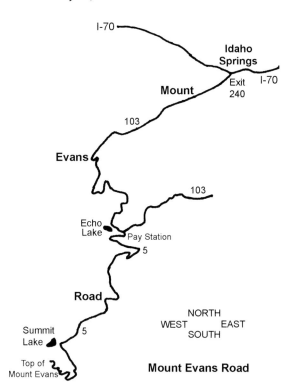

Great Sand Dunes National Park

The Great Sand Dunes are a remarkable place for producing dynamic images. The sand dunes photograph well year-round with late afternoon and sunset providing the best light. Consider shooting the dunes from a distance in the late afternoon, perhaps including sagebrush and mountains in the composition. For evening and sunset, move on foot into the dunes. I usually climb one of the taller ones to look around and determine the evening's subject. Hiking into the dunes does require physical exertion and may not be worthwhile if it's windy as the sand finds its way into everything. You may wish to bring a compass and flashlight in case it gets dark before your departure. I've also found that morning shooting can be productive from near the parking lot and along Medano Creek; however, because of mountains directly to the east of the dunes, they don't receive the various red hues of early morning light. **Directions**: From Colorado Springs, drive about 90 miles south on I-25. Exit at Walsenburg and follow U.S. Hwy 160 west, approximately 65 miles, over La Veta Pass and into the gigantic San Luis Valley. At the intersection of State Hwy 150, turn right (north) and follow about 15 miles to the park.

Sand Dunes

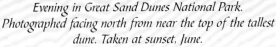

*Evening in Great Sand Dunes National Park.
Photographed facing north from near the top of the tallest
dune. Taken at sunset, June.*

Upon entering the park, make the first left past the visitor center; follow for about one mile to a large parking lot. Hike west, crossing the shallow Medano Creek and into the dunes.

If you're heading to the dunes during the warm summer months, I recommend a stop at **Zapata Falls**. It's a great place to plop your feet in icy water and cool off. To actually see the falls requires that you wade a short distance into a rock cut. To find

Zapata Falls from the entrance to the Great Sand Dunes, head south about 7 miles on State Hwy 150. Turn left at the well-marked road to the Zapata Falls parking lot. This gravel road is passable by all vehicles. From the parking lot, it's a short one-half mile walk up a gradual hill to the falls.

Morning at Great Sand Dunes National Park

Photography Tip: Split-neutral density filters are particularly useful for creating natural looking images during sunrise and sunset. They help prevent overexposing the sky or underexposing the darker portions of the image. To learn more about split-neutral density filters see pages 130-132.

Crystal Mill

Crystal Mill or Crystal Powerhouse as some people refer to it, is located along a four-wheel drive road about 6 miles east of Marble. This is another frequently photographed and published location. The rustic building sits on a rock face above a rushing mountain river surrounded by aspen. The lighting is best in the afternoon. Interesting perspectives can be found along and in the river downstream of the falls.
Directions: From Carbondale, drive State Hwy 133 south toward Redstone. Stay on 133 through Redstone; just before you start climbing up McClure Pass, turn left on Forest Road 314 (paved road) towards Marble. You'll reach the town of Marble in about 6 miles; stay on Forest Road 314 as it winds left and right through town. As you leave Marble, you will pass Beaver Lake on the right; followed by a steep hill. At the top of the hill, veer right at the junction of the road to Lead King Basin. You'll pass a small lake (Lizard Lake) on your left.

Crystal Mill

The road then curves left, heads downhill, becomes narrow, rough and has a steep drop on the right. For a few hundred yards, there is only enough room for one vehicle. If you have a passenger, you might want to send him/her to the bottom to hold traffic while you descend. **Note**: Four-wheel driving rules require vehicles traveling downhill to back up and yield the right-of-way to vehicles traveling uphill. Be very careful through this section as some vehicles have lost control and dropped over the edge. At the bottom of the hill, the road becomes much easier. Drive about 2.75 miles further until you reach the large parking area for Crystal. The only building remaining is the mill, which is immediately across the river. See the map on page 43.

Ashcroft - Ghost Town

Situated along a paved road near Aspen, Ashcroft is one of Colorado's finest examples of a high-country ghost town. This old mining town has many erect buildings and countless photographic opportunities. Autumn is one of its most photogenic seasons due to the high mountains and abundant aspen forest surrounding this historical little town. **Directions**: From downtown Aspen, head north on Colorado Hwy 82. When you reach the traffic circle (roundabout), enter it and take the Castle Creek Road exit. Follow Castle Creek Road south for about 10 miles; Ashcroft will be on the left. There is a $3.00 (donation) fee for access. See the map on page 43.

Ashcroft Ghost Town, September midmorning.

Hanging Lake

I include this location because of its unique arrangement of a beautiful waterfall dropping into a blue-green lake, and it's conveniently located along I-70. I think two things are required to make a great image here: heavy flowing water and green leaves on the foliage around the falls. Consequently, the best time of the year for shooting is late May through mid-July. For this location, I prefer the diffused lighting of a cloudy day. (Don't forget to keep the sky out of the composition.) You'll want to avoid direct sunlight in your photograph, as it will create hot spots and shadow areas that will be too dark. If you don't have a cloudy day, get to the shore of the lake early in the morning or late in the evening for the best lighting. While you're there, be sure to go just a tad further upstream and see spouting rock.

Directions: Traveling east on I-70, about 10 miles east of Glenwood Springs, take exit 125 (Hanging Lake exit). Only eastbound traffic can access the parking lot for the trailhead, so if you're westbound, go past it and use exit 122 (Grizzly Creek rest area), then head east on I-70 and use exit 125. This will lead you right to the trailhead parking lot. The hiking distance from the trailhead to Hanging Lake is about 1.2 miles. It's a steep

Hanging Lake Waterfall

(elevation gain is over 1,000 feet) and rigorous climb, especially when you're rushing to get the best light.

Hanging Lake

North Clear Creek Falls

f you find yourself traveling along Colorado Highway 149 between Creede and Lake City, be sure to investigate North Clear Creek Falls. I like to photograph here on overcast days or early morning and late evening when the sun is not shining directly on the falls. **Directions**: See Map on page 59. Turn off highway 149 onto Forest Road 510 (well-signed). This will be a right turn if you're traveling toward Lake City. Follow just a little more than one-half mile and turn left into the parking lot for the waterfall. There's no hiking required, but finding a suitable composition might necessitate some exploration of the area. **Note**: To find this waterfall on your more detailed map, first locate Spring Creek Pass; it's the southerly one of two passes along highway 149 between Creede and Lake City. From Spring Creek Pass, head about 6.5 miles south and turn left onto Forest Road 510. If the waterfall is marked on your map, you should see it indicated near this intersection.

North Clear Creek Falls

Photography Tip: Use a polarizer when shooting waterfalls. Compose your shot, then put on a polarizer and rotate it. You'll notice the shine on wet rocks surrounding the waterfall will disappear, allowing for better contrast between the waterfall and surrounding rocks. To learn more about polarizers see page 128.

Rifle Falls

This beautifully lush, triple waterfall is worth the visit for anyone traveling along I-70 between Grand Junction and Glenwood Springs. The mist created by the thunderous waterfalls offers the surrounding area a constant supply of water, transforming the landscape into a tropical-like oasis of moss-covered rocks, green grasses and leaves. If you especially enjoy photographing waterfalls, you should consider this location. It photographs well in both morning and evening when direct sunlight is not shining on it. It also photographs well at midday when direct sunlight is found evenly lighting the entire waterfall and surrounding area.

Directions: Take I-70 to Rifle; exit the interstate at Rifle, heading north on CO Hwy 13. Follow for about 3 miles, then turn right onto Colorado Hwy 325, and drive about 10 miles to the entrance of Rifle Falls State Park. There is a $3.00 to $7.00 entrance fee to the park. After entering the park, proceed through the campground to the picnic area parking lot. Park here and walk the few hundred yards to the waterfall.

Rifle Falls - Midday

Garden of the Gods

Garden of the Gods is an incredible city park in Colorado Springs. It's not actually a garden; it's a natural park, located on the west side of Colorado Springs. Garden of the Gods offers dramatic red sandstone formations that are very photogenic alone; however, compositions often include majestic, snow-capped Pikes Peak in the background. The rock formations are photogenic regardless of the season, however during the months of July, August and September, Pikes Peak is often without snow and does not enhance compositions. The best lighting occurs at sunrise and during the first 30 minutes thereafter. I strongly recommend scouting locations throughout the park in advance of shooting. It has both paved and dirt trails. Most of my shooting is done along the dirt trails and ridges. As you scout, bear in mind that it's the eastern side of the sandstone formations that will photograph best at dawn. The park is not that large and roads circle through it making scouting relatively easy. **Note**: The Park Service has many areas off limits for revegetation. **Directions**: From I-25 in Colorado Springs, take exit 146 and head west on Garden of the Gods Road. Follow to its end ("T" intersection) at 30th Street; turn left (south) and go about 1.5 miles. The visitors center will be on the left and the park entrance on the right.

Garden of the Gods viewed from the Visitor Center, midmorning, October.

Map of Garden of the Gods

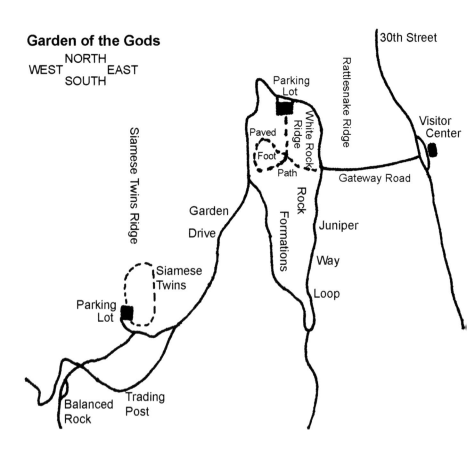

Some ridges are not named, however, I've named them here for easy reference.
Caution: Rattlesnakes inhabit Garden of the Gods.

Kissing Camel Formation

Location - This tree is located on top of White Rock Ridge toward the southeast. See the Garden of the Gods map for ridge location. **Note**: Sections of this ridge may be closed for revegetation.

Kissing Camels formation framed by a juniper tree,
Garden of the Gods. Taken midday, March.

Juniper Formation

Location -This tree is located on top of White Rock Ridge toward the southwest. See the Garden of the Gods map for ridge location. **Note**: Sections of this ridge may be closed for revegetation.

Reaching juniper tree and rock formations, Garden of
the Gods. Taken early morning in August.

Siamese Twins Formation

Location - This formation is found on one of the Garden's many dirt trails; only about a 10-minute hike. See the Garden of the Gods map.

Siamese Twins formation, Garden of the Gods. Taken early morning in January.

Gateway Formation

Location- This tree is located on Rattlesnake Ridge, north of its midpoint. See the Garden of the Gods map for ridge location. There is a dirt trail, running the length of this ridge, which directly passes the tree on the west side of the trail.

Gateway formation, Garden of the Gods. Taken at dawn, June.

Garden of the Gods

Location - This was photographed from the top of White Rock Ridge facing south. See the Garden of the Gods map for ridge location. **Note**: Sections of this ridge may be closed for revegetation.

Garden of the Gods, taken early morning in August.

Balanced Rock

Location - This is a very popular tourist location. Sunrise produces the best light and least amount of traffic. **Note**: This image was photographed kneeling in the road. (See the Garden of the Gods map for Balanced Rock location).

Balanced Rock, Garden of the Gods. Taken at sunrise, May.

South Gateway Rock Formation

Location - This tree is located on top of White Rock Ridge toward the southeast. This is the same tree used to frame Kissing Camels. See the Garden of the Gods map for ridge location. **Note**: Sections of this ridge may be closed for revegetation.

South gateway rock formation framed by a juniper tree. Taken at sunrise, August.

Juniper Tree on Siamese Twins Ridge

Location - The Siamese Twins formation can be reached by a short hike; about 10 minutes on a dirt trail. See the Garden of the Gods map for location. To find this tree, hike about 15 minutes further up the ridge on the trail running north of the Siamese Twins.

Juniper tree on Siamese Twins Ridge. Taken at sunrise, January.

Pikes Peak Framed by Siamese Twins

Location - This formation is found on one of the Garden's many dirt trails; only about a 10-minute hike. See the Garden of the Gods map for location.

Pikes Peak framed by a hole in the Siamese Twins formation. Taken early morning in January.

Landscape Photog

aphy Instruction

Photography Workshop

Landscape Photography Instruction

Now that you know where to take great landscape photographs in Colorado, the following instructional information will help you capture the images you desire.

Andy Cook and workshop participant in Rocky Mountain National Park.

Light

We use vision to detect a limited spectrum of electromagnetic radiation called light. The curious thing about our vision is that often we see what we think we should see For example, white paper looks white in both incandescent and natural lighting. However, light produced by an incandescent bulb has a greater percentage of long wavelengths (oranges and reds) as compared with daylight. We have a hard time distinguishing when a light source changes or shifts and offers additional shorter or longer wavelengths because our brain constantly adjusts our perception to make what we believe is white to appear white.

Film, on the other hand, is sensitive to any change in the predominant wavelengths. Take a photograph using outdoor film inside at night with a subject lit by incandescent light and you'll notice a predominat orange hue. Outdoor film is formulated to make images taken in daylight approximate what you see. While your brain can compensate and make white appear white in both incandescent light and daylight, film can't.

Film responds to subtle shifts in the wavelengths of light. Light at sunrise and during the first hours of the day, and again at sunset and during the last hours of the day, is the best light for landscape photography. During these times, the sun is low on the horizon and light rays are traveling through more atmosphere, which has a tendency to scatter and block the shorter wavelengths (blues) and allow the longer wavelengths (warm colors) to pass through. While your eyes may not notice this shift, film will readily record these pleasing, warmer tones.

Time of day plays a significant role in the outcome of an image. The noon shot of Tomichi Creek on the left is bland and uninteresting, while the sunset shot on the right is dramatic and interesting because of the lighting. The quality of light available is as important as the subject in landscape photography.

Exposure

Exposure is the amount of light acting on the film. As photographers, one of our challenges is getting the right amount of light to act on the film. We do so by using correct combinations of aperture size and shutter speed. We make incremental adjustments to aperture size and shutter speed in units called stops of light (plural) or a stop of light (singular). What is a **stop of light**? It is the amount of light required to either increase by double, or decrease by half the current amount of light. To gain or go up two stops of light is to receive four times more light than you started with. Conversely, to lose or stop down two stops of light is to receive four times less light than you started with.

Aperture - The adjustable opening inside the lens between the glass at the front of the lens and the glass at the back is the aperture; on SLR's, it is measured in "f-stops". The aperture is adjusted using a mechanical iris similar to the iris in our eyes. As a ring on the lens is turned, the opening inside the lens enlarges or contracts depending upon the direction the ring is turned.

The aperture scale and shutter speed scale are broken down in stops. Whenever you go up or down the standard increments of either scale, you gain or lose stops of light one stop at a time. On the aperture ring of your lens, if you move from one number to either the next higher number or next lower number, you've either lost or gained one stop of light. That scale looks like this:

Big opening   1.4 - 2 - 2.8 - 4 - 5.6 - 8 - 11 - 16 - 22 - 32 - 45   **Small opening**

A move from 2 to 2.8 is a one stop move. A move from 11 to 16 is a one stop move.
A move from 11 to 8 is a one stop move. A move from 2 to 5.6 is a three stop move.
With aperture, the smaller the number, the larger the opening and the more light
there is, and the larger the number, the smaller the opening and the less light there is.
Therefore, a move from 2 to 2.8 is is a one stop loss of light. A move from 11 to 16
is also a one stop loss of light. A move from 11 to 8 is a one stop gain of light. A
move from 2 to 5.6 is a three stop loss of light.

f-2.8; Aperture set at 2.8

f-16; Aperture set at 16

Shutter Speed

Shutter speed - The amount of time the shutter is open allowing light to reach the
film is the shutter speed. It is measured in seconds such as 1, 2, 4... or fractions of a
second such as 1/30 or 1/1000. In comparing shutter speeds, 1/60 will let in only
half as much light as 1/30. Longer shutter speeds may be necessary in low light
situations; however, longer shutter speeds may not freeze your subject's motion,
resulting in some blur. Similarly, we cannot hold our cameras completely still, so at
longer shutter speeds, the slightest hand movement can cause blur. As a general rule,
avoid shutter speeds slower than the "focal length" of your lens. For example, with a
standard 50 mm lens, 1/50 sec. is about the slowest shutter speed you should use to
hand hold your camera. With a 200 mm telephoto, avoid shutter speeds slower than
1/200 sec. When a slower shutter speed is required, be sure to use a tripod. More
serious photographers prefer to use a tripod for every shot regardless of shutter
speed — it's well worth the effort to avoid blurring your images.

The shutter speed scale looks like this:

2 sec - 1 sec - 1/2 - 1/4 - 1/8 - 1/15 - 1/30 - 1/60 - 1/125 - 1/250 - 1/500

Slow shutter speed   **Fast shutter speed**

Some cameras may have more or less numbers at either end of the scale. A move from one shutter speed to the next, up or down the scale, is a one stop move. Moving down the scale is moving to a longer (allowing more light in) shutter speed, 1/4 sec. to 1/2 sec. to 1 sec. Moving up the scale is moving to a shorter (allowing less light in) shutter speed, 1/15 sec. to 1/30 sec. to 1/60 sec.

The difference in **film speed** is also separated by stops of light. The common film speeds (ISO's) are 25 - 50 - 100 - 200 - 400 - 800, where the difference between adjacent speeds is one stop of light. Slow films are denoted by a lower number while faster films are denoted by larger numbers. A 200 speed film requires half the light for proper exposure compared with 100 speed film. Slower films have finer grain structure, allowing for sharper images and better enlargements.

Equivalent exposures (the same amount of light exposed to the film) can be achieved using various combinations of aperture size and shutter speed. For example, assume a shutter speed of 1/250 sec. with an aperture setting of f-8 gives the correct exposure. In that case, all of the following combinations will give equivalent exposures:

Shutter speed	Aperture
1/60	f-16
1/125	f-11
1/250	f-8
1/500	f-5.6
1/1000	f-4

The "**Sunny 16 Rule**" is an easy exposure rule to remember: Very simply, the rule states that on any bright, sunny day without clouds or haze blocking the sun and with a subject that is medium tone (see section on metering), larger than a camera bag, and front lit, your estimated exposure will be the shutter speed closest to the ISO of your film @ f-16. For example, if you're shooting with 100 ISO film, the shutter speed will be 1/125 sec. @ f-16; if you're shooting with 50 ISO film, the shutter speed will be 1/60 sec. @ f-16, or any equivalent exposure. For this rule to work properly, you must be shooting during midday light, approximately 10 a.m. to 2 p.m.

Depth of Field

Depth of field refers to how much of your image in terms of distance is in focus. When a lens is focused, there is actually a range of distances in focus, depending on the size of the aperture selected. With smaller apertures (f-16, f-22), more of the foreground, mid-ground and background will be in focus creating greater depth of field. Conversely, with larger apertures (f-1.4, f.-2), less distance within the picture will be in focus creating shallow depth of field.

Nikon 50 mm lens at f-1.8
Shallow depth of field

Nikon 50 mm lens at f-22
Greater depth of field

Why select one aperture setting over another? If your subject is wildlife in motion or a wildflower blowing in the wind, you'll select a large aperture to get a corresponding fast shutter speed. This will enable you to freeze the subject's motion while avoiding blur. In other cases, you may select the smaller aperture setting to achieve greater depth of field; very common with landscape images.

Lens selection also has an effect on depth of field. As a rule, the shorter the lens, the greater the depth of field for each aperture setting and focusing possibility. In other words, you can obtain greater depth of field with a 24 mm lens than with a 50 mm lens; however, you'll sacrifice subject size if you shoot the photograph from the same location.

Metering (film cameras)

Metering is used to determine the proper combination of aperture setting and shutter speed to expose the film to the appropriate amount of light. Cameras utilize the reflected light, or light coming off the subject, for metering purposes. They may sample light from various sections of the image. Typically, there are three options: 1) **Spot metering** - All of the metering is done utilizing the light in the very center of the viewfinder. 2) **Center weighted** - Other portions of the frame are considered, though the majority (70 to 80%) of the light measured is around the center of the viewfinder. 3) **Matrix metering** (Nikon), **Evaluative metering** (Canon) - Light entering at numerous locations of the image is used in more or less equal consideration.

1 some of the more expensive cameras, there is an extensive database of potential
nages and the presumably correct way to expose them. These cameras look for
ood comparisons between what you have in your viewfinder and what is in the
atabase to help determine the proper exposure.

Here's the big trick of metering (film cameras)

our camera can make the wrong exposure decision for a scene. Yes, it's true! The
amera meter can be fooled because of the way they are designed to function. They
ample the light in the viewfinder and no matter how bright or dark the scene is,
ley adjust the aperture and/or shutter speed so that the light exposes on the film as a
nedium tone. This means bright, white snow (light tone) is darkened to gray, drab
now (medium tone); and a black bear (dark tone) filling most of the frame will be
ghtened to a grayish, medium tone. That's how it works — it's that simple. So if
ou are shooting a medium tone such as a green forest, grass, northern blue sky
vithout sun, gray tree bark, gray rocks, deer, elk, etc., then your camera's metering
ystem in auto mode will set the aperture and shutter speed to properly expose the
lm. Manufacturers design their metering systems this way because they want the
najority of shots taken with their cameras to be acceptable; since most photographs
re taken of medium tone subjects, the majority are satisfactory. So if your camera is
ι the manual mode and you wish to shoot a medium tone subject, simply shoot the
ibject as your camera's metering system indicates. Additionally, if the same light is
ιlling on a medium tone object as is falling on your subject, which is not a medium
ine, you may simply take a meter reading of the medium tone object, then
∗compose and shoot your subject without any additional adjustments.

ow can you get the proper exposure when the subject is not a medium tone and
iere isn't one to meter on? Simply override your camera's decision and either let in
nore light (overexpose) or less light (underexpose) than your camera has determined
ecessary. If your camera is in the auto mode, you can do this by adjusting your
ompensation dial (see your manual), or set your camera to the manual mode and
nanually adjust it.

In this series of photographs, metering was done by spot metering on the snow on the right
side of the mountains in the background. The left photograph was exposed as a medium tone
(as the camera indicated it should be exposed). The center photograph was metered, then
opened up one stop (overexposed according to camera's meter by one stop). The right
photograph was metered, then opened up two stops (overexposed according to camera's meter
by two stops.) Which one do you prefer?

Manual Mode

The manual mode is recommended because in addition to properly metering your subject, you can adjust both shutter speed and aperture for desired effects, such as the blurring or freezing of motion. If you're in the manual mode and the subject is a field of snow, but there are no medium tones to meter, what do you do? Simple — get a meter reading for the snow and let in more light than your camera recommends. You may do so by choosing a longer shutter speed or wider aperture (opening up). Your camera will indicate that you are overexposing the scene, but ignore this and proceed because you want white snow, not gray snow. How much extra light do you need? If you want detail in the snow, open up one to two stops; for white without detail, open up two and one-half stops. Practice this and discover your preference. In summation, if you are shooting a light subject, you will need to overexpose the film, according to your camera's metering system, to get the proper rendition of the subject on film.

What about the black bear? Shooting in manual mode, your camera will give you readings that will turn the bear gray or lighter. You want him black, so you need to let in less light (underexpose). To do this, get the meter reading your camera wants, then underexpose by choosing a smaller aperture or faster shutter speed (stopping down). After doing so, you will notice your camera is indicating that an underexposure will take place — ignore it. How much should you underexpose? One to two stops will retain some detail in his fur; at two and one-half stops, the detail will blacken out.

The following is a scale to help you with tones. Using the color Green:

+2&1/2 stops open - burned out green
+2   stops open - extremely light green
+1&1/2 stops open - light light green
+1   stop open - light green
+1/2   stop open - dark light green
  Medium   Medium Green
-1/2   stop down - light dark green
-1   stop down - dark green
-1&1/2 stops down - dark dark green
-2   stops down - extremely dark green
-2&1/2 stops down - blocked-up / blackened out

This is a scale for slide film which sees only about five stops of light. That is two and one-half stops on each side of medium tone. **Note**: Print film can see about ten stops of light, five stops on each side of medium tone.

Once you've properly metered for a portion of the scene, the rest of the scene will fall into the proper tonal range. For example, let's say you've metered the grassy meadow in the foreground as a medium tone; by doing so, the snowy, white mountains in the background will properly record as a light tone.

To complete the discussion on metering, we must recognize that photographers often spend a lot of money buying a camera and then expect it to be able to do most or all of the metering. Some top of the line cameras can do it all; however, you may still wish to select the aperture or shutter priority mode to create desired effects, such as maximum depth of field or freezing motion. Other cameras may meter the vast majority of scenes correctly and only botch a few. It is advantageous for you to experiment with your camera and learn its abilities and limitations. If you know your camera will meter a particular scene correctly, then it may be beneficial to flip it to the aperture priority mode and concentrate your energy on composing the photograph.

Calibrating your camera meter

This calibration should be done with slide film.

a) Find a medium tone subject. Consider buying an 18% gray card at a photo store.
b) Set the ISO dial for the film you are shooting, then shoot one frame.
c) Now adjust the ISO dial up one notch to the next point on the dial and shoot another frame. Note that the next notch may not be the next common ISO film number.
d) Repeat step (c) until you have gone three notches above and three notches below your starting point.
e) After the film is developed, pick the slide that you consider to be properly exposed. The ISO notch used when that slide was shot is the proper ISO notch to use when shooting that particular film in your camera.

Remember to keep your eye in the viewfinder or close the viewfinder if possible to block light from entering and corrupting the readings).

Composition

What does a great outdoor photograph have that snapshots do not? Superb composition! It is an image that catches the eye of the viewer and evokes an emotional response, preferably the one intended by the photographer. There is a huge difference between taking snapshots and photographs. When taking snapshots, we tend not to scrutinize subject placement or evaluate complementing or distracting elements. Yet when taking photographs, we pay careful attention to every aspect of the composition. Composition is subjective in the choice of subject matter, location and perspective. However, there are guidelines that can lead you down the path to improved composition.

The Basics of Composition

In photography, composition is the arrangement of elements (mountains, streams, lakes, flowers, etc.) in the viewfinder that will create an image. Your goal is to make this arrangement as captivating and pleasing to the eye as possible. The following tips will help you achieve greater success.

Use the **rule of thirds** as a starting point for your composition. Imagine there's a tic-tac-toe grid in your viewfinder. Position your main subject in the viewfinder, at or near the intersecting points of the tic-tac-toe grid. Landscape images with the main subject centered in the frame are rarely appealing.

Avoid placing the subject in the center of the frame. In this photograph, both foreground and background subjects are in the center (left to right) of the frame, producing an awkward balance in the image. Also, the apparent haze gives a washed-out look, eliminating any possible color saturation.

Use leading **diagonal lines and curves** to draw the viewer's eye into the image and to the main subject; for example a log in the foreground leading out into a lake, a stream or a fence. Lines are powerful compositional components that readily attract the eye's attention; they should be used carefully. Every time you see a line in your viewfinder, evaluate it and only include it if you're certain it enhances your image.

The slowly curving stream is a powerful compositional component that draws the viewer's eye into the frame. If possible, have your lines and curves originate in the corners of the frame to create a more powerful effect.

Watch for the amount of **negative space** in your composition - too much will create an imbalance where the eye drifts off the main subject to the void of nothingness, and too little can squeeze the composition, reducing its impact and balance. A little extra negative space can be useful; often magazine covers will utilize the negative space of an image for a header or advertisements.

The empty, gray sky across the top of this image is an example of too much negative space. This composition would be far more pleasing if the sky were blue with fluffy, white clouds.

Consider the camera's **orientation (vertical or horizontal)**. One may be better than the other, so be sure to consider both. If selling your images as stock, having both orientations may be a good business decision (verticals are used for covers which generally pay higher amounts). **Note**: You may have to recompose to make the image work.

Mount of the Holy Cross. Which one do you like better? Why?

Try **framing** the subject with a simple arrangement of interesting components around or beside the main subject, such as between trees, branches of a tree, flowers, etc. Use simple framing components so they don't distract or interfere with the main subject.

Tetons framed by fence and gate.

Keep your **horizon level**, especially when working with horizons that are level in nature, such as oceans, seas, large lakes and deserts.

Add something to the **foreground**. Landscape and scenic photographs are greatly enhanced by placing an object such as a flower, tree stump, rocks or trees in the foreground. They add a sense of depth to the image. Be certain that both the foreground and the main subject are in focus.

Look for **patterns in nature**, such as ripples in sand, curving wood grain, water ripples, a stand of trees, etc. They often create an appealing image all by themselves.

Stones on a beach often produce interesting patterns.

It is very important to evaluate your subject from a **variety of possible angles**. Before placing the camera on the tripod, walk around while looking through the viewfinder; get on your knees or climb the hill behind you before deciding the best angle for an interesting shot.

After deciding what to shoot, take a look at the subject again. Is there a **picture within a picture**? Try changing lenses, or if you use a zoom lens, change the focal length to see if another pleasing composition unfolds.

Try to **avoid including white skies** in your compositions as they're generally uninteresting and distracting.

If the sky above were blue, this would be a far more interesting image. The colors blue and yellow complement each other.

See the effect when the white sky is cropped out. Do the sunflowers alone provide the most interesting and eye-catching photograph?

Consider **perspective**. If you're shooting flowers or animals, try shooting them from their level to create a more intimate image.

Looking directly down on flowers or animals is rarely appealing because it's the angle we commonly see them from. An image of a flower or small animal taken from its level is far more interesting. How often do we crawl on the ground to view flowers?

Keep It Simple !

In your viewfinder, search out and eliminate distracting elements; they compete with the main subject by drawing your eye away from the focus of your photograph. Try not to include everything in a scene, rather capture the essence of the scene with a few of its main components. Composition is often improved by thoroughly eliminating as many unnecessary elements as possible.

Identify your subject and eliminate all distracting elements. Zooming in on the tree and eliminating the second ledge of snow cleans up the composition and creates a more pleasing image. The viewer should not have to guess your subject; they should be able to identify it as soon as they look at the photograph.

As a rule, most people perceive the visual world from a standing height of four to six feet. Rarely, even when on vacation, do we get down on all fours and crawl on the ground to get a better view. Consequently, you can make images that are interesting and different by simply shooting from a lower or higher vantage point. Another note on perspective would be to consider which one best translates the emotional response you have to the scene. By lowering your perspective to the ground, you may create the effect that the subject is more dominant in the surroundings. By going to a higher vantage point, the subject may seem more inclusive in the surroundings.

The **tripod** is perhaps the most important tool in helping photographers improve compositionally. After you find the angle and composition you desire, place a tripod under your camera. This gives you the freedom to **slowly** consider every factor (lens selection, metering, composition, depth of field) of the shot before tripping the shutter.

It is important when shooting landscapes to photograph something that stirs an emotion. It can be a field of wildflowers, a small cascade or a grand waterfall. Ask yourself, "Would I spend $300.00 to matte and frame this for my wall?" If the answer is "no," save your film. Even when the answer is "yes," the image can still fail. Beautiful scenery doesn't necessarily translate into photogenic scenery. Only by shooting and honestly critiquing your photographs will you begin to produce images with better compositions.

Critiquing Photographs

Critiquing

Critiquing photographs is an effective way to develop your eye for composition. On the following pages are 5 images that we will critique together. Critiquing is a subjective exercise where disagreement is commonplace. Don't be alarmed if you disagree with my assessments.

Study the image.

Image 1a

What's wrong with it?

What could improve it?

Are there distracting elements?

Study the image.

Image 2a   What do you think?

Study the image.

Does anything detract from the
composition?

Image 3a

This image really needs more flowers in the box. The box is half of the image, but nothing exciting is happening in it.

Image 1b

Does your eye linger on the shadow in the bottom left of the image? Mine does. The mountain is supposed to be the background subject. Does it succeed? I don't think so. Would the clear, blue sky look far more interesting with clouds? Yes.

Image 2b

Did you look at the bright spot on the far canyon wall? I did. Is it intended as a compositional element? No. Bright and dark spots attract our eyes; therefore, if they exist in an image, they should be major compositional elements.

Image 3b

Study the image.

Image 4a

Can it be improved?

How?

Study the image.

Image 5a

Does something seem awkward?

Would a small change make a difference?

What?

I feel there is too much negative space in the bottom left of the image and the top drifts back to a mountainside, which I struggle to interpret. I can't see it clearly and my eyes keep searching the top of the image for more.

Image 4b

The image below is a better composition of this subject.

Image 4c

Where the fence enters the frame (dead center) is disturbing. It would be far better for the fence to enter the frame in the bottom right corner.

Image 5b

Image 5c

Image 5d

Photography Eq

ipment

East River, Crested Butte

Filters

Filters are critical in producing fine photographic images. They are often necessary for capturing an accurate representation of what you see. Why? Because film has a limited ability to record varying light intensities. Slide film can properly record about 5 stops of light — that's 2 & 1/2 stops on either side of medium tone. On the other hand, your eyes can perceive a much larger range of light intensity before reaching their limits; your eyes see 12 to 14 stops of light. Therefore, filters are often necessary to faithfully record a scene or produce a desired effect.

The following filters are very useful for landscape photography:

1. Polarizer - Many acceptable manufacturers.
2. Split Neutral Density Filter - I prefer the ones made by Singh-Ray.
3. Warming Filters - 81A or 81B (B is stronger than A). Many acceptable manufacturers.
4. Color Intensifier - I prefer the ones made by Singh-Ray (1-800-486-5501)

Polarizer

In many lighting situations, using a **polarizing filter** will help you increase the color saturation of an image. It does so by removing the shine or glare from non-metallic reflective surfaces such as water, glass, smooth leaves, rocks, etc. Once the shine or glare has been removed, the color of the object becomes more apparent and will record with richer tones on film. Polarizing filters are also used to cut atmospheric haze, resulting in skies with deeper blue color and increased contrast with clouds. Also, the elimination of haze allows more detail in distant compositional elements such as mountains, sea shore, etc.

Bear Lake

Bear Lake in Rocky Mountain National Park without polarizing effect. Notice the washed-out sky and haze in front of the distant mountains.

Bear Lake with same settings and polarizer rotated for maximum effect. Notice the richer colors throughout the image.

To use a polarizer, attach it to the front of your lens, then spin it until the desired amount of polarization is achieved. A word of caution with some slide films — too much polarization can result in an unrealistic dark blue or black sky. Maximum polarizing effect will occur when you are shooting perpendicular to the sun's rays. Stated another way, maximum polarization occurs when the line "camera to subject" is perpendicular to the line "sun to subject". There is virtually no polarizing effect when you are shooting directly toward or away from the sun (parallel to sun's rays). Other angles with the sun's rays will yield some polarizing effect. Be careful when using a polarizer on wide-angle lenses; one area of the sky might darken significantly more than other areas, creating an unnatural effect.

Circular Polarizer

Polarizing filters typically block about two stops of light. If you are using the metering system in your camera, put the polarizer on before metering for your shot, then meter in your usual manner. Both linear and circular polarizers are available. Linear polarizers may hinder a camera's auto focus and auto exposure abilities. Circular polarizers are a little more expensive, but will work with any camera system.

Split-neutral Density Filter

How many times have you photographed a blazing sunset or sunrise only to be disappointed with the resulting image? Either the sky was overexposed and washed out, or the foreground was underexposed and black. What happened? The range of light intensity in this type of scene often extends beyond the film's latitude (range of light intensity film can faithfully record). Human eyes can perceive about 12 to 14 stops of light before reaching their limits, a much larger range of light intensity than print film (about 10 stops) or slide film (about 5 stops). When photographing in these types of lighting situations, split-neutral density filters will help you control the light intensity in specific areas of the frame so you can record the scene on film exactly as you see it. Generally speaking, split-neutral density filters may be useful when a portion of any image is more than two stops brighter than other areas of the image.

A split-neutral density filter is a filter where one half is clear and the other half is tinted with a neutral, (doesn't impart a color) light-filtering tint. The tinted portion usually blocks one, two or three stops of light, depending upon the strength of the filter. They are easy to use — simply position the tinted side of the filter over the brightest portion of the image while placing the clear section of the filter over the darker area of the image.

These filters decrease the amount of light which passes through their tinted portion. They may have either a "feathered" or "hard" edge. (Edge line is where the tinted portion meets the clear portion.) The feathered edge provides a gradual change from the tinted portion to the clear portion, while the hard edge provides a more abrupt change. I carry a Singh-Ray hard edge, 2-stop, split-neutral density filter in my bag at all times. I use the rectangular version slid into a holder which attaches to the front of my lens. The holder allows me to not only rotate the filter, but also to move it up and down, allowing greater flexibility in proper placement of the tinted portion.

Split-neutral density filter

Split-neutral density filters are particularly useful when you have a dark line across the length of the image. This dark line may exist in the area where the sky meets the ground in the classic sunset or sunrise scene, and is important in hiding the edge line of the filter. If the edge line is noticeable, it will appear unnatural and be distracting to the viewer.

Without split-neutral density filter on left, with filter on right. Sunrise at Odessa Lake in Rocky Mountain National Park.

To meter for proper exposure when using a split-neutral density filter, follow these steps:

1. Meter the highlight area.
2. Make your normal compensations for lighting situation and subject matter.
3. Compensate for the strength of the filter by opening up one, two or three additional stops (depending upon filter strength used).
4. Insert the filter placing the tinted portion over the highlighted area and expose the film.

Or:

1. Meter the darker area of the image.
2. Make your normal compensations for lighting situation and subject matter.
3. Insert the filter placing the clear portion over the darker area and expose the film.

Note: Because the darker area of the image will be covered by the clear portion of the filter, this procedure does not require you to compensate for the strength of the filter. To avoid overexposing highlights when using slide film, follow the first procedure.

Filter holder (upper right). Adapter ring (bottom). Lens with adapter ring attached (upper left).

Filter holder attached to adapter ring which is screwed on the lens.

Filter in filter holder.

Color Intensifier

The color intensifier works great for enhancing a color that is not quite up to par, such as fall colors past or before peak. The intensifier I use enhances orange, yellow, red and any mix of them. I recommend the intensifier manufactured by Singh-Ray, because it seems to do the best job of leaving the other colors (white, green, blue, etc.) unchanged. Other brands of intensifiers, also known as enhancing filters, tend to cast an excessive reddish hue to the entire image. This hue is usually very pronounced in clouds and other light objects such as tree bark.

Without intensifier

With intensifier

Warming Filters

Warming filters are useful for removing a bluish tint which occurs when your subject is lit by the blue sky, not with direct sun (i.e. flower or animal in the shade). Your eye will not detect the blue tint, but film will record it. A warming filter simply counteracts this blue tinting effect. The filters come in varying strengths with (A) being the least and (C) having the strongest effect. Actually, if you want to purchase only one, I recommend getting the 81B.

Fairy slipper in shade without warming filter.

Fairy slipper in shade with warming filter.

Tripod

Don't just buy one, use it! I cannot stress this enough. This is the most important piece of equipment, especially for those trying to learn composition. A tripod is a must for clear, sharp photographs. Your hand cannot hold a camera still enough, especially when shooting slower films, macro or telephoto.

At practically every photography workshop I hold, participants struggle to gain familiarity with a piece of equipment that they've owned, but seldom used. Oftentimes, they are using the wrong kind of tripod, resulting in broken equipment and missed opportunities as they fret with adjustments.

What is a proper tripod for landscape photographers? An important feature to look for is a tripod with legs that do not attach to a center post. Many landscapes require shooting from uneven ground, hillsides and other precarious places.

The most suitable tripod for these varied surfaces is one with legs that move independently and can lock in a variety of positions out to 90 degrees. You will also be best served by a tripod that can adjust very close to the ground and support a camera at standing height without having to crank up an extension shaft. Another useful feature is a quick-release head, allowing you to simply pop the camera on and off with a spring-loaded snap or a flip of a finger. The tripod head should tilt to hold the camera in vertical format.

A common mistake to avoid when using a tripod is premature camera attachment. Photographers often approach a location, extend the legs of their tripod, secure their camera, and start shooting. Remember, the most interesting shots are often found from ground level or half-way up a hill twenty yards back. Before attaching the camera to the tripod, explore the area and experiment with different angles, heights, locations, vertical vs. horizontal, etc.

A quick-release head provides easy attachment and detachment of the camera.

Use a tripod like the one on the left. Avoid tripods with arms that attach to a center post.

Tripod legs should swing out independently and approximately 90 degrees.

Cable Release

A **cable release** (electronic or mechanical) will help you avoid shaking the camera as you trip the shutter.

Reflectors

Reflectors are useful for lighting a subject that is hidden in a shadow. They are used by shining the reflected light on the subject you wish to shoot, then taking your meter reading. They come in silver and shades of gold, creating the same effect as a warming filter.

Gold Reflector

Lenses

For landscape photography, you will find having a 24 mm, 35 mm, 50 mm, 70 mm, and possibly a 100 mm lens to be a handy selection to carry. Note: A quality zoom lens may help you cover this range and more in an affordable way. To shoot wildlife, you will find that having at least one lens that is 300 mm or larger is usually necessary.

This 28 mm to 200 mm zoom lens is an affordable way to cover a wide range of focal lengths and a light weight option for lengthy hikes. This lens also has macro capabilities.

Extension Tubes

Extension tubes may be used for macro work. They allow you to get closer to the subject, therefore magnifying it.
You simply attach the tube to your camera in the same manner that you attach a lens. Then you attach your lens to the tube just as you would attach it to the camera. By moving the lens further away from the film plane, the extension tube changes the focusing ability of the lens in such a way that you can get closer to a macro subject and still focus.

Rose focused as closely as possible with a 28-200 lens.

Rose focused as closely as possible with the same lens and an extension tube.

Diffusers

Diffusers are useful for shooting an object such as a flower in harsh daylight. You must hold it close enough to the subject so that the subject glows with the diffused light. Holding it too far away will only create a shadow. Diffusers quickly fold down and store in a small carrying pouch.

When using a diffuser, don't hold it too high above the subject as it will cause you to cast a shadow on your subject. Note that the darkness of my body's shadow and the diffuser's are comparable.

For the diffuser to work properly, it must be as close to the subject as possible. Note the soft light, not shadow, under the diffuser. Be careful not to include the diffuser in the image.

Paintbrush photographed in harsh midday light.

Paintbrush photographed at midday using a diffuser.

Discussions among photographers often revolve around equipment used. Below is a list of what I faithfully carry in my pack. Brand names are mentioned for the readers' convenience, but not meant as an endorsement of particular manufacturers.

Equipment List

* **Pack** - Lowepro Nature Trekker
* **Tripod** - Manfrotto 3021BPRO (tripod), Manfrotto 3030
          (tripod head)
* **Camera Body** - Nikon F4
* **Lenses** - Nikon 24 mm
          Nikon 50 mm
          Nikon 28 - 105
          Tamron 200 - 400
* **Filters** - Cokin Circular Polarizer
          Singh-Ray Color Intensifier
          Singh-Ray Gold-N-Blue Polarizer
          Singh-Ray Split-Neutral Density (ND-2G-HS)
          Singh-Ray Split-Neutral Density (ND-1G-HS)
          Singh-Ray Split-Neutral Density (ND-1G-SS)
          Tiffen 81B (warming filter)
          Cokin P series filter holder and adapter rings for each lens
* **Cable Release** - About 20 inches long
* **Extension Tube** - Nikon PK-13 27.5 mm
* **Flash** - Nikon SB-28
* **Flash extension cord** - Nikon SC-17
* **Clean handkerchief**
* **Lens Cloth**
* **Lens cleaning fluid and lens paper**
* **Spare AA batteries**
* **Black ground cloth**
* **John Shaw's Pocket Field Guide**

*
*
*
*

Check List

Here's a checklist of items to consider before you trip the shutter release. It's lengthy, but with practice, most of the items will become automatic and take only seconds to complete.

* Is there film in the camera?
* Is the ISO dial set to the correct speed?
* Is the film advancing?
* Is the compensation dial set properly?
* Have you selected the correct mode
    (manual mode or one of the program modes)?
* Is the camera in the correct metering mode
    (spot, centerweighted, or matrix)?
* Have you metered for the scene?
* Have you selected the correct aperture for the depth of field you
    desire?
* Have you focused properly?
* Have you selected the correct shutter speed to properly freeze or
    blur motion?
* Are you using a tripod and cable release?
* Have you considered the need for a filter
    (split-neutral density, polarizer, warming, color intensifier)?
* Have you checked for lens flare?
* Are jet condensation trails in the scene?
* Have you checked all of the edges and corners of the frame for
    distracting elements?
* Are you keeping the composition simple?
* Is your subject immediately apparent?
* Are all other compositional elements enhancing?
* Have distracting elements been removed?
* Is there too much or too little negative or empty space?

    *

    *

    *

    *

    *

Trip Log and Notes

This area is intended for you to keep notes...

Location:

Date:

Notes:

Location:

Date:

Notes:

Location:

Date:

Notes:

Location:

Date:

Notes:

Location:

Date:

Notes:

Acknowledgments

feel fortunate to live in a place as wonderful as Colorado. It has provided immense pleasure to visit and photograph locations throughout the state. During my travels, I am constantly impressed with the friendliness and welcoming nature of Coloradans. I'd like to thank the people whose paths I've crossed for their warmth and hospitality.

I'm particularly grateful to Richard Norman, a talented photographer and excellent instructor, who introduced me to landscape photography and whose brutal critiquing sessions accelerated my learning.

I especially want to thank my family for being patient with me during this project. It was consuming and I obsessed with it, drawing play time away from my daughters Meredith and Maggie and companion time from my wife Kati. - A.C.

Contact:
Andy Cook
Rocky Mountain Reflections Photography, Inc.
2518 Pine Bluff Road
Colorado Springs, CO 80909

For information on field workshops with Rocky Mountain Reflections Photography, Inc., visit their website at www.rockymountainreflections.com.

About the Authors

Andy Cook is an avid outdoorsman and gifted landscape photographer. He graduated from the State University of New York at Binghamton in 1985 with a B.S. Degree in Geophysics. He moved to Colorado in 1987 and immediately took to exploring the state. Upon discovering landscape photography, he embraced it with a passion. He thoroughly enjoys helping others develop their photographic abilities and experience the great outdoors. He considers Colorado a treasure to be shared with those who appreciate natural scenic beauty.

Andy has been published in numerous magazines and newspapers. His work also appears on postcards, note cards, and has been purchased by galleries in California, Colorado and New York, including The Metropolitan Museum of Art (NY).

"...Andy Cook is one of Colorado's best outdoor photographers."
The Voice, Fort Collins, CO

Andy Cook

Shar Scofield is a writer, editor and photographer based in Colorado. As an avid outdoorswoman, she captures the creative wisdom of nature as an art form to uplift and inspire the human spirit. Her diverse experience in both natural and corporate settings led to the creation of her company, Echoes and Images, which offers a product-line of inspirational, humorous and personalized magnets and cards.

Shar Scofield